PORTRAITS OF THE PAST

The Industrial Heritage of Old Monmouthshire

Chris Barber & Michael Blackmore

BLORENGE BOOKS
Abergavenny

Llanfoist Wharf, Brecon & Abergavenny Canal.

'The extraction of iron had hitherto depended upon the employment of charcoal. It was the fortunate discovery of coal in 1740 and the application of the steam engine to manfacturing purposes, that brought about a revolution in industrial methods and laid the foundations of Monmouthshire's commercial prosperity.'

G. W. Wade 1909

First Published 1996

Revised Edition 2001

ISBN 1 872730 05 1

Blorenge Cottage, Church Lane, Llanfoist,
Abergavenny, Gwent NP7 9NG.
Tel: 01873 856114

Typeset by Chris Barber
Designed By Chris Barber and Michael Blackmore

Printed by MWL Print Group Ltd
Units 10-13, Pontyfelin Ind. Est., New Inn, Pontypool, Gwent NP4 ODQ.
Tel: 01495 750033

CONTENTS

List of Illustrations   6
Foreword   7
Introduction   9
Pontypool - Home of South Wales Ironmaking   12
Blaenafon Ironworks   17
Following the Iron to Llanfoist Wharf   23
Ironmaking in the Clydach Gorge   38
Ironworks from Nantyglo to Rhymney   45
Wye Valley Ironmaking   67
Other Monmouthshire Furnaces & Forges   74
The Canal Age   85
Railroads and Tramroads   101
Coal Mining in Monmouthshire   111
A Passion for Steam   125
Stone and Steam in the Black Mountains   152

Museums and Visitor Centres   162
Locations of Sites   163
Recommended Reading   163

Acknowledgements   164

Text by Chris Barber & Illustrations by Michael Blackmore

LIST OF ILLUSTRATIONS

Water outlet at Garnddyrys	1
Llanfoist Wharf, Brecon & Abergavenny Canal	2
Goytre Lime Kilns	8
The Blorenge and Llanfoist Bridge	11
Capel Hanbury	13
Pontypool Park Gates	14
Pontypool Park House	15
Blaenafon Ironworks	17
Stack Square and Balance Tower	18
Hallelujah Lampost, Blaenafon	21
North portal of Pwll-du Tunnel	22
Map of Blaenafon and Garnddyrys	24
Limestone Checker's Cottage, Blaenafon	25
Puddler's Arms near Garnddyrys	26
Lamb and Fox Inn, Pwll-du	27
Hill's Tramroad at head of Cwm Llanwenarth	28
The slag 'Monster' at Garnddyrys	29
View across Cwm Llanwenarth	30/31
Reconstruction of Garnddyrys Forge	32
Detail of plateway and fixing method	33
Plan of Garnddyrys Forge and Rolling Mill	33
Hills Tramroad above Cwm Craf	34
Llanfoist Incline	35
Llanfoist Wharf, scene from *Rape of the Fair Country*	36
Entrance to Llanfoist Tunnel	37
West side of Clydach Gorge	38
Reconstruction of Llanelly Furnace	39
Reconstruction of Clydach Ironworks	40
East side of Clydach Gorge	41
Clydach Ironworks from old painting (1808)	42
Smart's Bridge, Clydach	44
Crawshay Bailey	47
Reconstruction of Ty Mawr complex	49
Round Tower at Ty Mawr	51
Ebbw Vale Steel Works	55
Abraham Darby	56
Sirhowy Ironworks	59
'St David' Locomotive at Tredegar Ironworks	60
Bedwellty House, Tredegar	61
Iron clock tower, Tredegar	62
Cefn Golau cholera cemetery, above Tredegar	63
Remnant of furnace at Blaen Rhymni	64
Bute Town houses, near Rhymney	66
Angidy Ironworks and worker's houses	69
Coed Ithel blast furnace, near Llandogo	73
Reconstruction of Abercarn blast furnace	75
Typical scene on Brecknock & Abergavenny Canal	85
Monmouthshire Canal at Allt yr Yn	87
Section of the 14 Locks at Pensarn, High Cross	88
Junction Cottage at Pontymoile basin	91
Stop Gate on Brecknock & Abergavenny Canal	92
Reconstruction of Goytre Wharf	93
Construction of Clydach Aqueduct	94
Reconstruction of Gilwern Wharf	95
Loading timber at Gilwern Wharf	96
Aqueduct at Govilon	97
Llanfihangel Tramroad at Govilon	98
Typical scene on Brecknock & Abergavenny Canal	100
Example of a plateway	101
Example of an edge rail	102
Typical tramroad scene	103
Clydach Railroad at Gilwern Aqueduct	104
Map of Monmouthshire & Breconshire Tramroads	105
Llanfihangel Tramroad Bridge at Llanfoist	107
Llammarch Railroad	108
Child labour underground	112
Sinking a new shaft	113
Collier at Big Pit	115
Big Pit, Blaenafon	117
Cwmbyrgwm water-balance gear	119
Pumping engine house at Glyn Pits	120
Pit head gear at Big Pit, Blaenafon	122
'Tornado', Britannia Class Locomotive	126
Castle Class locomotive at Abergavenny	128
Castle Class Locomotive at Llanfihangel	129
Railway boundary marker	130
Locomotives at Brecon Road, Abergavenny	131
Evening train, Brecon road, Abergavenny	132
Govilon Station c.1950	133
Gelli-felin tunnels on M.T. & A. line	134
Clydach Lime Works	135
Railway viaduct at Clydach	135
Llanelly Quarry sidings	136
LNWR 0-8-0 'Super D' loco at Tafarnaubach	137
GWR station at Ebbw Vale	139
Crumlin Viaduct	143
Tintern Station, Wye Valley Railway c.1950	145
G.W.R. Employee at Tintern Station	149
Brunel's iron railway bridge, Chepstow	151
Grwyne Fawr Valley	152
'Duckinfield' locomotive	153
'Anita' locomotive	154
'Brigg' locomotive	154
Map of Grwyne Fawr railway	155
View from dam wall	155
Grwyne Fawr quarry	156
Construction of Grwyne Fawr Dam	157
Travelling to work	157
Blaen y Cwm Village	158
Opening Day Special, 1928	159
Locomotive at Grwyne Fawr Dam	160
Family at Tintown	160

FOREWORD

All those interested in the heroic industrial past of the old County of Monmouthshire (later Gwent) - and who is not - must owe a real sense of gratitude to Chris Barber and Michael Blackmore who have done so much to bring it alive for us. To many of us Chris Barber is well known for his books encouraging and emboldening us to explore some of the wildest corners of South East Wales. Fortunately for the industrial archaeologist the drift of modern heavy industry towards the coast has left many former industrial sites surrounded by areas of peace and great beauty. Where once the din of hammers drowned all other sounds and coal dust turned the very sheep black, we can hear the bird song and enjoy the beauty of woods and open moorland

I have known and admired Michael Blackmore's scholarly and meticulous reconstructions of old industrial sites for many years and am confident that this attractive volume will bring his work to the notice of an ever widening circle of admirers. With many of the sites described, Michael Blackmore's illustrations of what remains, or his reconstructions of what is gone, serve to fire our imaginations and deepen our understanding in a way that nothing else could achieve.

Monmouthshire in the 17th and early 18th centuries counted for almost all the iron produced in Wales and for about thirty years in the mid 18th century Pontypool had a virtual monopoly in the United Kingdom of the production of tin-plate. One of the unsolved mysteries of early industrialisation is the site of the first production of tin-plate in Wales, whether at Pontypool or at nearby Pontyfelin. The surviving documents do not help - perhaps one day excavation will provide the answer, As the industrial revolution gathered momentum and new sources of iron and coal were developed along the line of what is now the Heads of the Valleys road, so ironmaking tended to slip across the county boundary into Glamorgan, where for a time Merthyr Tydfil was the largest town in the Principality. It is all the more important, therefore, given the preponderance of Cardiff in modern Wales, that we should be reminded of the part that Monmouthshire once played in providing the sinews for our country's greatness and in developing the world we now inhabit. I hope and trust that the readers of this work will be inspired to visit many of the sites described and illustrated and so familiarise themselves with places much better known to our ancestors and at the same time discover some of the most fascinating areas of our beautiful land.

Sir Richard Hanbury-Tenison
H.M. Lord Lieutenant for Gwent

Goytre Lime Kilns

INTRODUCTION

Before the Industrial Revolution, Monmouthshire was a pastoral and agricultural area where the western valleys were peopled with farming folk. Apart from crudely made looms and ingeniously contrived wooden machinery inside the corn mills, mechanical devices made of metal were almost unknown. The small amount of iron that was produced was made by smelting the ore with charcoal in little bloomeries, with the blast provided by portable bellows. But Monmouthshire was destined to become one of the largest iron producing centres in the world.

Several small ironworks were established at Pontypool, Monkswood, Abercarn and elsewhere in the county by Richard Hanbury, a London Goldsmith, around 1570. There is also a record of a furnace being established at Blaenafon in 1600 but its location has yet to be discovered.

During the early 18th century the Pontypool works became the largest producers of tin-plate in the country and as late as 1750 still dominated production of iron in South Wales, producing 1300 tons of pig-iron annually to 300 or 400 tons produced in Glamorgan and further west. All this was very soon to change to the disadvantage of Pontypool. The early works relied to a great extent on charcoal, and water was essential to power the bellows in the blast furnaces and the big hammers of the forges. The ideal site for these early ironworks was beside a fast-flowing river with large woodlands adjacent. The ironstone was obtained mostly by scouring and leaching while limestone was plentiful on the slopes of the western hills. The cutting and converting of charcoal was expensive, however, and constituted a brake on production.

In 1709 Abraham Darby of Coalbrookdale in Shropshire discovered that once the sulphur was removed from coal, it could be used in the form of coke which was a better fuel for smelting. But it was not until about fifty years later that coke was generally adopted as a fuel in other parts of Britain. The iron industry then rapidly went into a new phase of development. Between 1760 and 1840 a chain of ironworks was established along a narrow strip of hill country stretching for about twenty miles between Blaenafon (Monmouthshire) and Hirwaun (Glamorgan). They were situated in narrow valleys and thus separated from each other by hills. Close by were rich deposits of ironstone, limestone and coal which were the essential materials required for the iron making process.

The first ironmasters were from Staffordshire and the North of England and they exploited the mineral wealth of the 'Heads of the Valleys' of South East Wales to make it the most important iron making region in Britain.

In the early days of this industry the only form of transport between the iron works and the coastal ports was the packhorse. It soon became obvious that there was an urgent need for better communications and this resulted in the construction of canals, tramroads and eventually railways. In a very short time the valleys of Monmouthshire and Glamorgan became one of the most concentrated areas of British industry. People seeking work came in their thousands from the rural parts of Wales, England and Ireland, attracted by the possibility of employment or higher wages.

These once peaceful agricultural valleys now echoed with the roar of blast furnaces and before long their waste products were despoiling thousands of acres of land while the rivers which once sparkled and were alive with trout became little more than open sewers.

Overcrowded and insanitary living conditions led to disease in the rapidly expanding towns. In particular there were several outbreaks of cholera in some of the communities where people lived in ever increasing squalor, surrounded by rotting garbage tips and backyard piggeries, which resulted in contaminated drinking water.

The iron industry in South Wales produced a third of the total production for the United Kingdom and efficiency was increased through constant technological developments which resulted in a greater amount of iron being produced in each furnace.

An increase in the demand for ordnance resulted from the Napoleonic wars and the government showed

Opposite: *Goytre Wharf Lime Kilns.*

particular interest in South Wales for there was a good supply of mineral deposits in this area. However, at the end of the conflict with France, the price of iron fell suddenly from £20 to £8 a ton and the iron industry of South Wales went into sudden decline. But this was only a temporary setback for by 1840 the number of furnaces in blast had doubled since 1815.

Between 1801 and 1921 the population of the county increased from 45,000 to 450,000. With the influx of so many immigrant workers into the area, English became the main language in the valleys of South Wales although many locals still firmly clung to their traditions and continued to bring up their children to speak Welsh.

Today it is fascinating to study the birth of our modern industrial society with its associated evils of exploitation and social deprivation. The term industrial archaeology first appeared in print in 1955 in an article by Michael Rix, published in 'The Amateur Historian'. Four years later the Council for British Archaeology organised a National Conference to launch the subject. It embraces many aspects such as the study of the remnants of early blast furnaces and canal architecture. The Industrial Revolution was a period of inventive genius that led to fascinating technical developments and rapid growth in population and prosperity for the entrepreneurs.

The so-called industrial valleys of South East Wales now have a diversified economy with the development of light industries on industrial estates, but unfortunately unemployment is still a major problem in such towns as Tredegar, Ebbw Vale and Blaenafon.

The Valleys landscape has changed considerably with virtually every tip removed or re-shaped and landscaped. Large areas of sub-standard housing have also been replaced or renovated to meet present day standards and one is never far from attractive countryside with sweeping views.

Living in Llanfoist, beneath the looming bulk of the Blorenge I first began to take a special interest in the county's industrial heritage after walking impressive routes such as Hill's Tramroad. Following tracks across the bracken clad hillside, I ascended inclines, tramped along tramroads and inquisitively poked my nose into the long abandoned stone-lined tunnels. Then one day

I found myself imagining the characters in Alexander Cordell's moving novel 'Rape of the Fair Country', walking these same paths. I began to hear the sounds of horse-drawn trams, the roar of furnaces and the whine of the rolling mill at Garnddyrys.

Gradually the idea came to me to write a walking guide giving the historical background to locations mentioned in the novel. I contacted Alexander Cordell, who gave his agreement for the book to be entitled 'Cordell Country'.

I took many photographs of present-day scenes when I was preparing the book but soon came to the conclusion that what I really needed to bring it to life was a set of reconstruction drawings to portray sites as they looked in the nineteenth century. It was then that I decided to contact Michael Blackmore, a local artist with a remarkable talent for re-creating the past in very detailed pen and ink drawings. It is particularly relevant that Mike has a strong interest in industrial archaeology and participated in the Abergavenny Steam Society excavation of the Garnddyrys Forge in the early 1970s.

Also, like myself he has a special affinity with the Blorenge Mountain having experienced its changing moods throughout the seasons. It was the start of a much valued friendship and I am now delighted to once more have the opportunity of working with Mike on this new book which will provide a comprehensive appreciation and record of the industrial heritage of this fascinating County.

To enable us to tell the story of the industrial history of the entire County, as it was in the 18th and 19th centuries we have referred to it as 'Old Monmouthshire', with the adjective 'old' being used to avoid confusion with the new unitary authority which bears that name but only but covers eastern Gwent.

We have compiled *'Portraits of the Past'* to provide a tribute to the men, women and children of the Industrial Revolution who laboured on windswept hillsides, constructed tramroads, puddled iron, hauled trams, burrowed deep in the ground, extracting coal and toiled in so many other ways. This book should also help people to more fully appreciate the technical progress that was made in the space of a comparatively brief period.

Chris Barber
Llanfoist
1996

PONTYPOOL
HOME OF MONMOUTHSHIRE IRONMAKING

The story of iron-making in old Monmouthshire begins at Pontypool, which is a town sadly neglected by the majority of tourists for it has never been regarded as an inviting place to visit. However, it has much to offer and as a South Wales valley town, it is quite picturesquely situated.

Wedged into the bottom of a deep valley, from which the sides rise steeply on either side Pontypool stands beside the Afon Lwyd which was originally called the Torfaen ('breaker of stone'). This fast flowing river rises in the peaty moorland plateau known as Milfraen Flat, near Garn yr erw to the north west of Blaenafon and flows down the Eastern Valley to join the River Usk, 18 miles away, near Caerleon.

The Eastern Valley contains many memories and remnants of iron extraction, coal mining, limestone quarrying and also the various industries that once depended on these raw materials.

Visitors coming here for the first time should initially make their way to The Valley Inheritance Museum where a permanent exhibition tells the story of the valley and its people from the earliest times to the present day. The museum is housed in the Georgian stables of Pontypool Park House which was once the home of the Hanbury family who had their seat here for over 300 years and were the first major ironmasters in South Wales. Their stately home was surrounded by 158 acres of beautiful woodland.

Construction of the house was started in 1670 and it was completed by 1694. At various periods since then it has been extended and also rebuilt. In about 1820, in order to improve its amenities a forge which operated in the Park was closed and removed for it was obviously too close to the Hanburys' home for comfort.

In 1887, Pontypool celebrated the Jubilee of Queen Victoria by holding a huge fete in this park. Blondin, the famous dare devil was the star attraction and he crossed the arena on a hire wire riding a Pennyfarthing Bicycle.

Pontypool Park was acquired from the Hanbury family in the 1920s by a consortium of local authorities and made available for public recreation.

At the end of the Second World War it became the home of the famous Pontypool Rugby Football Club. The old house became a convent school operated by the Sisters of the Order of the Daughters of the Holy Ghost - a teaching order established in Pontypool in 1903.

At the Pontymoile end of the Park is a beautiful set of wrought iron gates. These were a present to Major John Hanbury from the Duchess of Marlborough on the occasion of his second marriage in 1703. Some 150 years later the gates and piers were in bad repair. The previous stone piers were replaced with cast iron substitutes and the gates themselves were put in order by Mr Deakin, a Varteg mining engineer. The new gate piers were made in Blaenafon, but the 1703 gates themselves are likely to have come from Derbyshire.

Although iron making on a small scale had long been carried on in the Eastern Valley, and also at Tintern under the supervision of the monks of that place, it was only with the arrival of Richard Hanbury that large scale exploitation of the mineral wealth of the area began. Richard Hanbury's partners at different times were his eventual son-in-law, Edmund (later Sir Edmund) Wheeler and his uncle, John Brode of Dunclent, Worcestershire. Neither of these, however, had any considerable stake in Hanbury's enterprises. Hanbury was in constant trouble over the Crown's interest in maintaining a supply of the best iron to the Tintern wire works, in which the Queen and many of her Council had shares, and the development of more profitable lines of trade. Nevertheless, by 1575, Hanbury was operating some six or seven ironworks in Monmouthshire and Glamorgan and even though constrained (after he and Edmund Wheeler had spent an uncomfortable three months in the Fleet Prison) to agree to supply the wire works with what they wanted.

Glyn Trosnant in Panteg parish and 800 acres of woodland in the parishes of Mynydd Islwyn and Panteg, was leased for a period of twenty years to

Edmund Roberts of Glamorgan, Richard Hanbury of London and Edmund Brode of Worcestershire.

In 1576 he had been able to secure a long-term supply of cordwood by leasing from the Earl of Pembroke (the land was later purchased) some 950 acres of wodland in the Gwyddon and Glyn valleys. The original rent was '21s and 32 sound oxen of reasonable size of the Welshe brecde'.

Richard Hanbury's furnaces were probably of a square or truncated pyramidal shape, reaching to a height of about 16-20 ft. The interior resembled the bowl of a smoker's pipe, some 6-7 ft. in maximum diameter, and was lined with sandstone. The hearth was also made of sandstone and was about 4 ft. square. Above it and on one side was another smaller aperture from which the molten slag or waste could be drawn. The continuous air draught to the furnace was supplied by leather bellows of tremendous size, about fifteen feet in length, and compressed alternately by strong cam arms fastened to a long cylindrical axle connected at right angles to a large water wheel which was turned by the rushing waters of a nearby river.

These furnaces were fed from the top with alternate loads of charcoal and the lightly roasted iron ores. Following the first three days preliminary heating, sufficient molten metal accumulated near the hearth and was drawn off every twelve hours into a long channel which had been scooped in the sandy floor with a triangular tool. When freshly fired, the amount of metal discharged into each mould was 500-700 lbs., but as the hearth of the furnace became enlarged by wear, the amount reached a weight of 2,000 lbs.

Although the output from the water-driven blast furnaces was considerably greater than that of the earlier bloomeries, and was attained with much less manual exertion, there were two disadvantages - large amounts of charcoal were consumed and the pig iron produced required an annealing heat treatment in special forges to render the iron sufficiently malleable for industrial and domestic purposes.

Pontymoel may be considered as the first place in Wales where ironworks of any size were constructed and the forge of those days was situated in the present Park adjoining the river opposite Trosnant, hence the name of the latter which means 'across the stream.

The ironworks at 'Old Furnace' in the Crumlin valley were formerly known as Glyn Trosnant and were about 2 miles from the centre of the town.

The next forge in Pontypool was in 'The Grove', that is the ground on the opposite side to the Park House. A road in those days ran through the site of the Park probably as far as the Town Bridge, from which Pontypool obtains its name.

Skilled men were brought by the Hanburys from their works in Worcestershire to supervise their operations at Pontypool and to undertake technical work while the local Welshmen were given jobs as puddlers and labourers.

The name of Bartholomew Pettingale occurs as clerk of the works in 1615. He was then aged 50 and his descendants remained for many years in this County. Francis Pettingale, for example was vicar of St Woolos Church, Newport from 1704 - 1726.

Major John Hanbury (1664 - 1734) was the pioneer of the tinplating industry and his agent Thomas Cooke of Stourbridge invented the rolling mill. The first one is said to have had stone rollers and it replaced the labour-intensive process of manually hammering out wrought-iron bars into sheets. The iron sheets, or blackplates as they were termed, were readily manu-factured into kettles, saucepans and other domestic articles for which there was soon tremendous demand.

Left: *Capel Hanbury was one of the earliest pioneers of the iron trade in South Wales. He was the son of a London goldsmith or banker. He settled in Worcestershire, but in 1588 purchased land at Pontypool and commenced the manufacture of iron.*

Born in Stourbridge, Thomas Cooke became the chief agent for the Hanbury interests in Pontypool. He lived at Upper Goitre in a house which he had built and it became known as Ty Cooke. His great-grandson founded the ironworks at Clydach in company with Edward Frere, father of Sir Bartle Frere. The tomb of Thomas Cooke can be seen in Trevethin churchyard.

Edward Llwyd the Welsh antiquary visited Pontypool in 1697 and later described the rolling machinery that he saw there:-

'One Major Hanbury of this Pont-y-Pool shew'd us an excellent Invention of his own, for driving hot Iron (by the help of a Rolling Engin mov'd by Water), into as thin Plates as Tin. But without a draught of the machine I cannot give you a notion of it. They cut their common iron bars into pieces of about two foot long, and heating them glowing hot, place them betwixt these iron rollers, not across but their ends lying the same way as the ends of the rollers. The rollers moved with water driven out these bars to such thin plates, that their breadth, which was about four inches becomes their length, being extended to about 4 foot, and what was before the length of the bars is now the breadth of the plates. With these plates he makes Furnaces, Pots, Kettles, Saucepans, etc. These he can afford at a very cheap rate (about the third part of what is usual').

Hammering was the only method of producing thin sheets of iron until 1695 when Major John Hanbury and his brilliant foreman, Thomas Cooke brought out an invention for rolling flat sheets of iron between what they called 'cylinders'. This enabled plates of smoother and more uniform surface to be produced in large quantities. It was the invention of rolls, first applied at Pontypool, which later established and gave impetus to the tinplate industry. At short intervals improved methods of pickling, annealing, cold rolling and tinning followed.

By 1736 tin-plates were being exported and at the end of the 18th century there were nine iron and tin-plate works in South Wales - four in Monmouthshire, two in Glamorgan, two in Carmarthenshire and one in Cardiganshire.

In 1783 Henry Cort devised grooved rolls for producing the bar iron, and during the following year he designed the reverberatory puddling furnace which simplified the process and improved the quality of wrought iron. He is regarded at the greatest benefactor of the iron trade but eventually died in a state of extreme poverty.

Right: *This beautiful set of wrought iron gates at the Pontymoile entrance to Pontypool Park are a reminder of the almost forgotten importance of this town as a world renowned centre of ironmaking.*

Watkin George, a well respected engineer at Cyfarthfa Works, Merthyr Tydfil, transferred his services to Pontypool in 1807, to remodel the whole of the works for Capel Hanbury Leigh. Puddling furnaces were erected at the Osborne Forge to produce iron known since as coke quality. At the Town Forge he introduced the Dandy Fire and Hollow Fire, both which inventions greatly improved the quality of the metal and increased output. The product was known as best charcoal quality.

At Pontymoel Watkin George also constructed a large water wheel for power purposes, modelled on the one at Cyfarthfa. On this site he also erected the mills and tannery house which remained in operation for about 80 years.

Around 1735, Pontypool became famous for the production of Japanware. This technique was developed from experiments with lacquer carried out by Thomas Allgood, a Northampton man who had been taken on as a manager at the Pontymoel works. A series of experiments had led him to the discovery of a method of applying a lacquer to tinplate that was both durable and inexpensive.

The Allgood process was not used until some years after his death in 1716 and his son Edward succeeded him as a manager. He hit upon a method of pickling blackplate in acid made from fermented grain to present a prepared surface for tin-plating or enamelling. Edward and his brother John subsequently set up a business in Trosnant to produce Pontypool Japanned ware in 1732

The earliest products were decorated in gold with Chinese subjects on a plain black, crimson or dark brown background. Snuff boxes and trays formed the main part of the early production.

The iron used for Pontypool Japan was the Osmond brand - already well known in the wireworks for its toughness, and the industry was carried on in some old cottages in Lower Crane Street between 1660 and 1822. Edward Allgood retired in 1760 and his sons continued the business for another year. But then a family argument resulted in two of the sons leaving to set up a rival factory at Usk, seven miles away, leaving their brother Thomas at Pontypool. Production continued at Pontypool until 1820 and West Place off Crane Street in Pontypool for long after was referred to as 'Old Japan'.

Left: The original part of Pontypool Park House was built for Major John Hanbury during the 1690s. It was extended between 1752 and 1765 with the construction of a low-fronted and taller addition behind the original house. Further improvements were made by Capel Hanbury Leigh who made extensions which were completed by 1810. This remained the Hanburys' family home until 1920, when the house and its grounds were given to the town.

The enamelling process was a secret of the Allgood family of Pontypool and Usk and produced a hard, brilliant, heat-resisting lacquer. The designs were rich and intense and included gilt effects - birds, flowers, figures and oriental landscapes. One of the stock embellishments of the Japan consisted of butterflies, and years ago the inhabitants of Usk were called 'butterflies' as a consequence. Among the designers was Benjamin Barker whose son Thomas became a famous artist. The Usk factory used a chocolate-brown ground with golden varnish, and also a transluscent crimson, applied directly onto the tinned surface.

By the end of the eighteenth century, the Hanbury Works and the Japan Works at Pontypool were world-famous, and Archdeacon Coxe even ventured to prophesy that Pontypool would soon become a second Birmingham.

When the last member of the house possessing the secret for making these remarkable goods suddenly died the industry decayed at once. Articles of Pontypool Japan are now highly prized by collectors, and examples can be seen at The Valley Inheritance Museum.

Ironmaking was carried out at Pontypool by the Hanbury family for nearly three centuries. In 1850 their works were leased to a Midland company and five years later to the Ebbw Vale Company which finally abandoned steel manufacture in Pontypool a century or so ago.

Development of the Iron Industry in Pontypool

1425	Iron first manufactured in the Pontypool area by David Graunt and his cousin Jeven'of Trevethin' who operated a small bloomery furnace on the banks of the Afon Lwyd.
1570	Cwmffrwdoer furnace is in operation by Richard Hanbury.
1576	Trosnant Furnace in operation.
1576	Pontymoel Furnace is erected by John True, a Sussex ironfounder from Robertsbridge.
1608	Death of Richard Hanbury, and his nephew John Hanbury takes over his South Wales industrial interests valued at £5,000.
1658	Death of John Hanbury.
1658	Capel Hanbury (son of John) purchases land and forges at Pontypool - which were previously leased. He enlarges the ironworks andacquires further extensive tracts of land. Output of the works is increased considerably.
1685	Capel Hanbury retires and his son Major John Hanbury, aged 21, takes over the management of the Pontypool works. He is assisted in his developments by Thomas Cooke of Stourbridge and Thomas Allgood a Northamptonshire man.
1697	Construction and development of the rolling mill to manufacture iron sheet (or black plate).
1734	Death of Major John Hanbury, and his third son Capel Hanbury takes over. Under his direction the works gains an international reputation for the quality of its rolled iron plates, tin plates, nails and wire.
1764	Death of Capel Hanbury.
1795	Capel Hanbury Leigh succeeds to the family estates. He updates the works and keeps the workforce employed until the late 1840s.
1812	Capel Hanbury Leigh enters into partnership with well known South Wales engineer Watkin George. during the Napoleonic Wars the Pontypool works reaches a peak of efficiency and prosperity.
1830	The partnership of C.H. Leigh and Watkin George is dissolved.
1840	The works is losing £10,000 a year
1850	Capel Hanbry Leigh sells off some of his industrial interests.
1851	A decision is taken to lease all the business interests to the Ebbw Vale Company, thus ending all the Hanbury connections which had lasted for two hundred and eighty years.

BLAENAFON IRONWORKS

Blaenafon Ironworks was established in 1789 by Thomas Hill and Thomas Hopkins who leased the land from the Earl of Abergavenny at a rent of £1,300 per year for a 21 year term. It cost £40,000 to build and in 1790 the furnaces started producing pig iron which was initially transported by mule to Newport. Six years later the Monmouthshire Canal was opened between Newport and Pontnewynydd. This was linked with the Blaenafon Ironworks by a six mile tram road down the Eastern Valley. The ironworks expanded rapidly during the Napoleonic wars and by 1815 it was the third largest ironworks in South Wales. The biggest were Cyfarthfa and Dowlais at Merthyr Tydfil.

Archdeacon Coxe came here in 1799 during his tour of Monmouthshire and described the scene as follows:-

'At some distance the works have the appearance of a small town surrounded by heaps of ore, coal and limestone and enlivened with all the bustle and activity of an opulent and increasing establishment.

The view of the buildings which are constructed in the excavations of the rocks is extremely picturesque, and heightened by the volumes of black smoke emitted by the furnaces. The coal is so abundant as not only to supply the fuel necessary for the works, but large quantities are sent to Abergavenny, Pontypool and Usk.

Although these works were only finished in 1789, three hundred and fifty men are employed, and the population of the district exceeds a thousand souls. The hollows of the rocks are strewn with numerous habitations, and the healthy ground converted into fields of corn and pasture.'

Thomas Hopkins died in 1789 and his son Samuel on inheriting a large sum of money decided to build a fine house for himself which he called Ty Mawr. It was referred to by local people as either 'The Big House' or 'Blaenafon House'. Samuel Hopkins was a popular man in Blaenafon and the town mourned his passing when he died in 1816. His sister Sarah constructed a school in his memory and frequently taught in it.

In due course, Thomas Hill's son who was also

Above: *This view through an archway in the wall of the casting house shows the remains of two of the blast furnaces at Blaenafon Ironworks. There were five furnaces in total and they were built into the hillside so that they could be charged from above.*

named Thomas, arrived in Blaenafon to help his father run the ironworks. This young man made quite an impression on the town with his extravagant lifestyle but he was also rather arrogant and soon became very unpopular. Drink and rich living shortened his life and by 1827 both of the Thomas Hills were dead. Then along came the next in line who was yet another Thomas Hill and he took on Robert Wheeley the works manager as his partner. They ran the concern together until 1836 when it was taken over by Robert William Kennard.

The works by now had expanded considerably and when the travel writer Nicholson came here in 1840 during his 'Tour of Wales' he described it as follows:-

'At the works of the Blaenafon Iron Company, five furnaces are all in blast, blown with cold air and six others erecting. This mineral property is one of the best and most valuable in the County of Monmouth, and these works have been distinguished for the superior strength and general excellence of their iron. These five furnaces produce about 400 tons of cast iron per week, and about one half of which is refined, and part of it made into cable iron, and the remainder is sold for tinplates and foundry work. This company is erecting extensive forges and rolling mills.'

Michael Blackmore's drawing shows the remains of two of the blast furnaces. At one time there were five in operation here. They were built into the hillside so that they could be easily charged from above. In the early days blast furnaces were worked with open tops, with the gases being allowed to escape into the air, and at night the whole neighbourhood was illuminated.

Stack Square was built in about 1789 to accommodate the skilled workers who had been hired from the Midlands. They lived in the two facing rows of four roomed houses. At a later date the central connecting terrace was constructed and the Company offices were located on the ground floor. On the upper floor accomodation was provided for single workers.

The Square takes its name from a 60 ft. high stack which once stood on the plinth which can be seen in the centre of the square and was connected to a steam engine which supplied the power blast for the furnace.

According to the 1851 Census, 84 people lived in the square and no doubt they were all employed by the Blaenafon Ironworks Company. As many as ten people lived in one of these small cottages and one couple actually raised no less than nineteen children here.

1843 was a disastrous year for the Blaenafon Company, summed up by the following comment in the Monmouthshire Merlin:-

'The present state of the iron-trade annihilates hope, we see nothing but ruin before us and behind us. The trade must refine within its proper limits, but how that is to be affected - who are to stand, who are to fall - what is to become of the unemployed - how starvation is to be arrested, and the ruin of thousands averted - are questions beyond our province to unravel, but which must be met boldly in our face because they are not to be avoided - they are already at our door.'

James Ashwell, a civil engineer, was appointed to build three new furnaces and blast engines and also the stone balance tower at the end of the furnace yard. However he spent so much money that the capital of the company soon vanished and the works came to a stop. Ashwell left for pastures new and the owners had to raise fresh capital. The works were then put under the management of Harry Scrivener who during his term of employment wrote a useful book entitled *'History of the Iron Trade'*.

Unfortunately the works still did not prosper and Mr. Scrivener was replaced in about 1847 by Richard Johnson, a brother-in-law of William Crawshay who owned the Cyfartha Ironworks at Merthyr Tydfil. But once again the works came to a stop and fresh capital had to be raised. The management was then placed in the hands of a committee consisting of Thomas Hill, Robert Wheeley and Philip Jones, a banker who represented the Herberts of Llanarth.

The Balance Tower was built in 1839 to provide a means of lifting loaded trams to a higher level. Pipes carried water into a container which by virtue of its own weight lifted a tram loaded with pig iron straight from the casting house to the top of the tower, from where it was transported by rail to Garnddyrys Forge. The water in the container at the bottom of the tower was then drained and the weight of the descending

Opposite: *A present day view of part of Stack Square which was built in about 1798 to accomodate skilled workers from the Midlands. In the foreground can be seen the remains of a plinth on which once stood a 60 ft high stack which was connected to a steam engine that supplied the blast for the furnaces. In the background can be seen the Balance Tower, constructed in 1839 by James Ashwell.*

dram returned the empty container back to the top of the tower.

The Blaenafon company shop in North Street near the Drum and Monkey Inn was owned and run by the Ironworks Company. This was the only shop in town and all the workers had to spend their hard earned cash there. Shopping was all done on credit which in due course was subtracted from the workers' weekly wages which were soon swallowed up and massive debts accumulated creating much bitterness and anger.

It used to be said that the world was girdled with Blaenafon iron and this was a reference to the great days of the Railway Age when Blaenafon was world famous for its superior quality iron rails which were in tremendous demand. Three other British foundries even had an arrangement with the Blaenafon Company that allowed them to stamp the impressive words 'Blaenavon Iron Co.' on their rails which was a certain way of ensuring a good sales record. But by 1870, Blaenafon had ceased to produce iron rails, for the works was not able to compete with the high quality Bessemer steel rails which by this time were being produced at Ebbw Vale.

In the late 1960's the National Coal Board sold the ironworks site to Blaenafon Urban District Council for land reclamation. Stack Square was declared unfit for habitation and the residents were rehoused. In 1972 the Department of the Environment took the site into their care and work started two years later on consolidating the remaining buildings with the intention of turning the site into a museum. The site is now under the care of Cadw: Welsh Historic Monuments, and is open to the public from Easter to the end of September. Special arrangements for party visits outside this period can be made by contacting the Torfaen Heritage Trust at The Valley Inheritance Museum.

Development of Blaenafon Ironworks

1789	Ironworks and Stack Square is constructed.
1790	Pig iron is being sold by the company.
1796	Tramroad to Pontnewynydd is completed.
1789	Death of Thomas Hopkins.
1795	Death of Benjamin Pratt.
1810	Nos 4 & 5 furnaces are put into blast.
1817	Garnddyrys Forge sends its first iron to Newport.
1824	Death of Thomas Hill.
1827	Death of Thomas Hill the younger.
1833	Blaenafon pioneers use of 'hot blast' in South Wales.
1836	Thomas Hill the third sells the company to the Blaenafon Iron & Coal Company for £220,000.
1839	Water Balance Tower is built by James Ashwell.
1840	Three new furnaces put into blast. James Ashwell resigns.
1841	The Blaenavon Iron & Coal Company is employing 2,002 people (this includes 135 boys and 36 girls under the age of 13 years).
1849	Coking ovens built.
1851	Census shows that 84 people are living in Stack Square.
1853	The hot blast process is adopted at Blaenafon.
1854	Monmouthshire Railway Co. open their line to Blaenafon.
1859	A new Forge and Rail Mill is opened at Forgeside.
1860c	Forge and Mill at Garnddyrys closes.
1861	Hill's Tramroad is abandoned.
1864	Blaenavon Iron & Coal Co. is liquidated and Blaenavon Company Ltd. is formed.
1868	First furnace at Forgeside is brought into operation
1870	Blaenavon Company sells out to the Blaenavon Iron & Steel Company Ltd.
1874	E.P. Martin is appointed as General Manager.
1876	Percy Carlyle Gilchrist is appointed works chemist.
1878	First steel is produced at Forgeside, Blaenafon.
1880	Introduction of the Bessemer process and a mill for producing tyres is built.
1898	Steelworkers from Blaenafon are employed in Russia to set up a Bessemer plant.
1904	No 1 blast furnace at the old works, which had been retained to produce cold blast iron is finally shut down.
1911	Blast furnaces at old works robbed of stone to build St James Church.
1938	Last furnace at Forgeside closes down.
1974	Ancient Monuments Branch of the Welsh Office takes Blaenafon Ironworks site into its guardianship.

The Hallelujah Lampost in Blaenafon was a popular place for political meetings in the 19th and early 20th centuries. It was known by this name because the Salvation Army band frequently used to play under it.

FOLLOWING THE IRON TO LLANFOIST WHARF

The best way to gain an understanding of the route taken by the trams laden with Blaenafon pig iron is to follow it on foot. Not only does this provide a fascinating walk, but one can also enjoy spectacular views across the Usk Valley. It is a walk that you will always remember and is best undertaken as a linear route with a car positioned at each end.

Leaving Blaenafon Ironworks, make your way to the Brynmawr road and then cross it to follow a tarmac lane leading up to two houses. After crossing a stile, ascend a short incline and then pause at the top to examine the remains of a braking device which once controlled the rate of descent of the trams.

As you continue along the track, you may enjoy wide views across to Coity Mountain and Big Pit. Below are the remnants of the village of Garn-y-erw and an area of hillside known as 'The Patches'. Nearly two centuries ago men dug here for the ironstone which was found embedded in the shale. The ironstone deposits were often removed by a 'scouring' technique. This involved extracting the minerals (which fortunately lay close to the surface) by first removing the turf and then clearing away the top soil by releasing water from a dammed pool above. When the dam was breached the water surged down and scoured the soil away to reveal the iron ore. About three tons of ironstone were required to make one ton of iron.

Ahead will soon be seen a stone stack, perfectly square and built of large blocks of dressed stone. This is the site of Hill Pits which were sunk in the late 1830s to meet the demand for ironstone and coal for the Blaenafon Ironworks. The twin shafts were filled in many years ago and originally the stone stack was linked with a boiler house.

Just past a shimmering pool turn right to follow a well defined incline heading up to the skyline. It was constructed by Company Engineer, Dyne Steel in about 1850 and is half a mile long. He laid four lines of rails and positioned an engine on top of the ridge to control four wire ropes which hauled the trams. Passing through a cutting to gain the crest of the ridge it is worth pausing to take in the extensive view across the Vale of Usk to the Black Mountains, while to the west the summits of the Brecon Beacons may be seen.

The incline on the far side of the hill has largely been destroyed by open cast operations but tracks lead down to the vanished village of Pwll-du (Black Hole). At one time about three hundred people lived in this windswept village. This was a lively and hardworking community where the men were employed as colliers, quarrymen and ironworkers. The quarrymen of Pwll-du provided the limestone that was used in the iron making process at Blaenafon. Their work was hard and dangerous and accidents were frequent. Excess limestone and coal were sent to Herefordshire and Breconshire.

A low archway, now bricked up, is the entrance to the Pwll-du tunnel which was constructed for the purpose of transporting coal and limestone from Pwll-du to the Blaenafon Ironworks. When the Garnddyrys forge came into operation it meant that on the outward journey the empty trams could be loaded with pig iron, thus making its use dual purpose. Unfortunately the route was single track and it became very congested, causing much wasted time and effort, and no doubt frequent accidents must have occurred. It was nearly one and a half miles long and the men who led the horse drawn trams must have cursed this subterranean route, for it was the longest tramroad tunnel in Britain. The tunnel follows a curving course of nearly two miles through Mynydd y Garn Fawr. It is stone vaulted at both mouths and is about 2 metres in height and width.

Near the mouth of the tunnel there used to be two rows of cottages. Long Row stood at the side of the tramroad and stretched out in the form of a slight curve from the tunnel mouth to an engine/winding house. On the other side of the tunnel mouth and at a higher level was Short Row and the whole community obtained their water from a spring near the tunnel entrance.

About fifty yards from the tunnel mouth, on its western side, were two groups of stable blocks, where the quarry ponies were kept. A partition down the centre of the main block provided stalls for six horses.

Three of the horses worked in the quarry, hauling tram loads of limestone up to the waiting trucks. Over the smaller stable block was accomodation for the ostler. This building was known as Tunnel House and a pond which was used to wash mud off the horses.

Opposite: The north portal of the Pwll-du tram road tunnel which was constructed to connect Blaenafon Ironworks with Garnddyrys Forge. It was nearly one and a half miles in length and the longest tramroad tunnel in Britain.

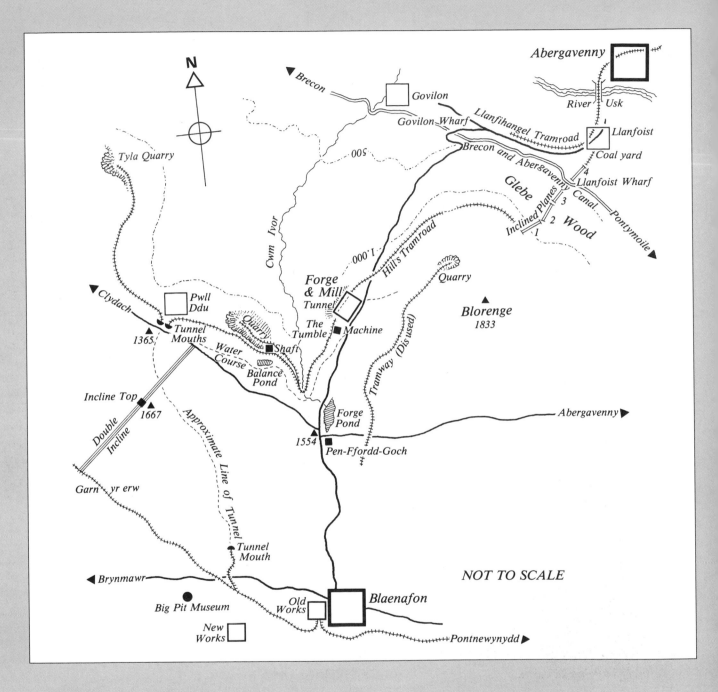

Above: *Blaenafon and Garnddyrys showing works and communications c.1865.*

Left: *The Lamb and Fox Inn is one of the highest public houses in Britain and once served ale to the people of the now vanished village of Pwll-du.*

There was also a Blaenafon Company shop here where the workers, who were paid in tokens, had to do their shopping. Adjoining Long Row was a chapel-of-ease known as St. Catherine's with the village school attached to it.

The old village hall of Pwll-du is one of only two remaining buildings of this once thriving village. It was built in 1940 after an initial levy of one penny per week on the locals provided a sum of £2,000 which was augmented by a grant from the collieries. It is now used as a weekend Outdoor Centre.

In 1960 the village was declared a slum and the first dozen families were moved out of their old stone cottages into new council houses which had been built for them at Govilon down in the Usk Valley.

The remainder of the people were moved out as further houses in Govilon became available, and the old villageof Pwll-du was then sadly demolished by Abergavenny Rural District Council.

There is one other old building that survived and more than thirty years later it is still occupied. This is the old Lamb Inn which has been restored by the landlord Brian Lewis. It had previously been kept as a pub by his parents but then remained closed for many years until Brian reopened it as 'The Lamb and Fox'.

From here a section of tramroad heads towards the Blorenge ariels which can be seen on the skyline. After crossing a rather boggy area, where there are stones to step on if you can find them, you will reach the site of the old Balance Pond.

Opposite: *The Puddlers' Arms on the Blaenafon to Abergavenny road was situated just above 'Fiddler's Elbow' and was much frequented by the Garnddyrys ironworkers.*

Left: *This strange looking mound of slag is known locally as the 'monster' and it stands near the site of the Garnddyrys Forge above Cwm Llanwenarth.*

The Balance Pond once held the water that was used to operate a lifting system in a shaft cut into the face of the Pwll-du quarry, directly below this point. The old pond is now just a long rectangular hollow lined with stone., It has not held water for many years, despite the fact that until recently the Ordnance Survey map (1:25,000 scale) showed it clearly as an inviting blue pool.

From the far end of the pond a track leads down to Hill's Tramroad (named after the Ironmaster Thomas Hill). Follow it towards Cwm Llanwenarth, taking care not to walk too close to the edge of the track, where a steep drop was once guarded by an iron rail. Pause at an opening in the trees and look across the valley at the site of the old Garnddyrys Forge and the scattered ruins of the workers' cottages. Michael Blackmore's drawing shows how the scene might have looked in about 1830. Billowing smoke rises from the tall chimneys of the puddling furnaces, where pig iron from Blaenafon was converted into wrought iron and a rolling mill produced the final products such as bars, rails and plates.

On reaching the head of the narrow cwm cross Rhiw Ifor, which was here long before the tramroads were even thought of, and then scramble across the stream where the old stone bridge that once supported Hill's Tramroad has disintegrated. Walk on past the ruins of a little stone building which once served as a blacksmith's shop (also referred to as the Tumble Beer House).

Stop here and look back at the convergence of tracks on the other side of Cwm Llanwenarth. Hill's Tramroad curves around to the top of Pwll-du Quarry and the lower track, which is now barely visible, leads to the foot of the quarry. Cutting diagonally down the hillside is the prominent path of Rhiw Ifor which provided the original route down through Cwm Llanwenarth.

The steep slope below the tramroad is known as 'The Tumble' and this name is said to recall the occasion when a certain Dic Shon tumbled a hundred feet down this steep bank and broke his leg.

Also to be seen are the ruins of Pwll-du Howard where the Garnddyrys Overman used to live in a privileged spot well away from the smells and noise of the Garnddyrys Forge.

Opposite: *Hill's Tramroad at the head of Cwm Llanwenarth where a small stone building probably served as a blacksmith's shop. This tramroad was constructed in about 1820. It ran from the mouth of Pwll-du tunnel to Garnddyrys Forge and then followed the 1200 ft. contour line to the steep north-east face of the Blorenge where it connected with three inclined planes descending to Llanfoist Wharf.*

29

Ahead now can be seen the slag 'monster' Unfortunately its head has been vandalised in recent years with the result that it no longer resembles a chicken, frog or squirrel, or whatever creature people usually saw in their imagination.

Beyond the pile of slag is the site of the Garnddyrys Forge. Situated at an altitude of 1,300 ft. it must have been a wild and windy place to work especially in mid winter. During a week's operation some 300 tons of finished products were turned out here. Iron bars and rails were produced to be transported to many parts of Britain and to various countries throughout the world.

An excavation was carried out on the site during the period 1971-73 by the Industrial Archaeology Group of the Abergavenny and District Steam Society. The small band of enthusiasts often worked here in winter conditions when freezing temperatures gave them some appreciation of what life must have been like for the ironworkers who laboured here during the early part of the nineteenth century.

Situated at such an altitude, this site is a most unlikely one for an industrial undertaking, and one may wonder at the daring and enterprise of the men who were responsible for such an endeavour.

The land for the forge site was purchased in 1817 from William Price for £7 and the following year the long strip of land for Hill's Tramroad to connect Garnddyrys with the canal at Llanfoist was acquired from John Hanbury Williams.

Above the site of the forge can be seen the outline of two ponds, which are now dry, but each cover approximately one acre in area. They were constructed to supply water to the steam engines which were in use on the site. An outlet can be seen in the retaining wall of the upper pond and this was the supply point to the workings below. In due course it was found that these two ponds were not large enough to supply sufficient water to operate both the forge and the rolling mill so another pond was constructed at Penfford-goch (better known as Keeper's Pond or Forge Pond) to provide additional water. A channel may also be seen contouring around the hillside carrying water from the old coal levels at Pwll-du to top up the Garnddyrys Ponds.

An interesting feature below the forge site is a short tunnel which was probably constructed to protect the tramroad from slag. There is a section of about 35 yards which can be entered with care.

The Garnddyrys Forge and Rolling Mill were only in use for a period of about 50 years and in 1860 the rolling mill machinery was dismantled and removed to a new plant at Forgeside on the Coity side of Blaenafon.

It may be assumed that Hill's Tramroad became redundant and closed at the same time.

A shareholders meeting was held on 22 April 1853 to decide the fate of the Garnddyrys Forge and the following extract is taken from the minutes book:

'The Works having now returned to a profitable condition the Directors have again seriously considered the best means of increasing the production of wrought iron, and at the same time of still further diminishing the expense of its manufacture. They are satisfied that this may be accomplished by the removal of the mill from Garnddyrys and its re-erection, with increased power and efficiency, on the Freehold Property of the Company at Blaenafon, and they desire to call the attention of the shareholders to their reasons for this conviction.

The site of the mill at Garnddyrys has been a constant cause of inconvenience and expense on account of its distance from the H.Q. at Blaenafon, and now that the Monmouthshire Canal Company have reduced their tonnages and improved the mode of conveyance along their road, these disadvantages are the more strikingly felt; the transit from Garnddyrys being by a circuitous and expensive route of twenty four miles, while the port of Newport will be reached by a locomotive railway from Blaenafon of only 16 miles.

The power of the present mill is scarcely equal to the production of 200 tons per week, it is thus proposed to make the new one, eventually, more than double that power say equal to 500 tons per week, this increase, while tending to reduce the cost of the common charges upon each ton made, will enable the company to enter more largely into the manufacture of rails.

Taking all these points into consideration the Directors have commenced this important alteration, as the means not only of increasing very materially the profit of the concern in favourable times, but what is of equally essential importance, of saving the company from losses in unfavourable years.'

Further on is the site of the Garnddyrys Square which consisted of twenty houses built on three sides of a triangle providing five, ten and five dwellings on each side. By 1870 they had been partly demolished. A separate block known as Garnddyrys Row was clearly shown on the 1827 one inch to one mile scale Ordnance map, but by 1938 they were abandoned.

Just beyond here, Hill's Tramroad is intersected by the Blaenafon Road and on the other side is the site of the Queen Victoria Inn which was frequented by folk from Garnddyrys. On Saturday night 3rd August 1946, the landlord Mr. F. Lewis was hosting a lively party to celebrate the completion of new improvements.

Above: *A view across Cwm Llanwenarth towards Gilwern Hill. To the right on the near side of the valley can be seen the mound of slag close to the site of the Garnddyrys Forge.*

A pianist was thumping out a lively tune on the piano and the bar was full of people dancing and having a merry time. At 10.15 p.m. precisely, when there were thirty people in the room, the floor suddenly gave way and everyone except one fortunate chap fell with the piano, into the cellar. The man who was left behind, was sitting on a seat that had been fastened to the wall and so he remained there stuck like a fly, looking down with astonishment at the people heaped on the floor below. Soon afterwards the inn was abandoned and eventually demolished.

Hill's Tramroad was constructed in about 1820. It ran from the mouth of the Pwll-du tunnel to Garnddyrys Forge and then followed the 1200 ft. contour line to the north side of the Blorenge.

Drivers controlled their downward descent by levering on a hardwood beam known as a sprag which locked the rear wheels when required. It was possible to achieve speeds of up to fifteen miles an hour, with a load of five tons of limestone aboard, while descending the one-in-twenty gradient down to the head of the Blorenge bowl.

The very early tram roads used L shaped rails, known as plateways, which were designed to guide smooth and non-flanged wheels (which were later developed for use on edge rails). Sleepers were initially cast iron but it was found that these were brittle and liable to snap. Then wood was tried for a while without a lot of success and so in due course rails were mounted on stone blocks using iron saddles or chairs which were fastened to the stone blocks with spikes driven into oak plugs inserted in the block holes. The L shaped cast iron plateway rails were 4 ft. long 3 ins. wide and chamfered to 2 ins. wide on the top running surface.

Benjamin Outram in 1799, recommended the use of stone blocks as sleepers and described the method of construction:

'The ground is first formed in the best manner the nature of it will admit, and perfectly drained: then covered with a bed of small stone or good gravel, six inches in thickness, and four yards in breadth, for a single road, and six yards for a double one; on this bed, stamped firm, are placed blocks of stone for sleepers for the rails; each block being upwards of one cwt.; in the centre of each block a circular hole is drilled six inches deep, and in it is put an octagonal plug of oak five inches long, which receives an iron spike, that fastens down the ends of the two rails that rest upon the block, the spaces between the blocks are filled with small stones, which are rammed close about the blocks, and covered with gravel, but not so high as the soles of the rails outside, nor so high as the top of the flanches on the inside between the rails...'

A shallow cutting leads to a tunnel (through which the more adventurous may pass with care). From the path outside the tunnel is a bird's eye view of the Vale of Usk and a wide panorama embracing the Black Mountains, Sugar Loaf, Skirrid Fawr and Skirrid Fach.

On the right of the track are the remains of a small building and a well constructed retaining wall. It was near here that a winch house was situated to control the descent of the trams down three inclines to Llanfoist Wharf.

The trams first descended to a collecting area (just above the present tree level) where the loads were re-sorted and the trams arranged in order of prority before being sent down the second stage of the incline which was known as 'The Big Drop'. Full trams descended under gravity pulling empty ones up on the other track. Accidents frequently occurred and were generally caused by badly loaded and runaway trams.

Spanish ore of high quality (70% - Blaenafon ore was only 26%) was brought from Newport by narrow boat to Llanfoist and then sent up the incline to Garnddyrys to pass through the Pwll-du tunnel to Blaenafon.

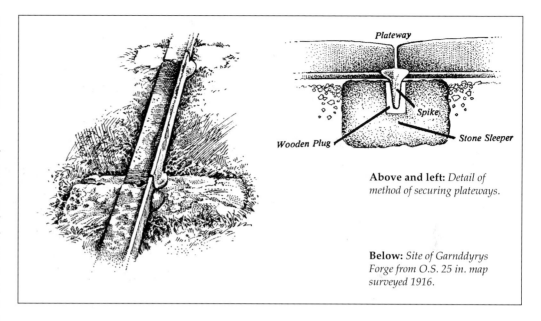

Above and left: *Detail of method of securing plateways.*

Below: *Site of Garnddyrys Forge from O.S. 25 in. map surveyed 1916.*

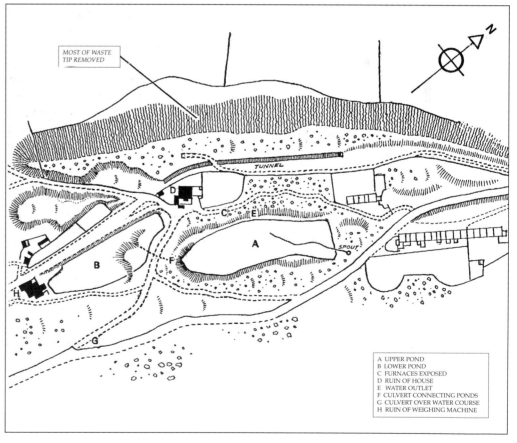

MOST OF WASTE TIP REMOVED

A UPPER POND
B LOWER POND
C FURNACES EXPOSED
D RUIN OF HOUSE
E WATER OUTLET
F CULVERT CONNECTING PONDS
G CULVERT OVER WATER COURSE
H RUIN OF WEIGHING MACHINE

Left: *A view looking down the Llanfoist incline which plunged steeply down the front of the Blorenge mountain. This section was known as the 'Big Drop' and at the bottom is Llanfoist Wharf on the Brecknock & Abergavenny Canal. Full trams descended under gravity pulling empty ones up on the other track. A brake wheel set in a pit at the top of the incline controlled the rate of descent of the trams.*

Opposite: *Hill's Tramroad near the top of the Llanfoist incline. The driver controlled the rate of descent along the gentle gradient of the tramroad by levering on a hardwood beam, known as a sprag, which locked the rear wheels when required. An experienced spragger could achieve speeds of up to fifteen miles an hour with a load of five tons of limestone.*

35

The ore later returned through the tunnel as pig iron en route to Garnddyrys for the next stage in the process to finally descend the incline as a finished product.

The first section of incline is not a right of way so a path is followed down through the fields to gain access to the top of the second incline. As you descend the knee jarring slope look out for stones with holes bored into them where the double line of rails was once secured. Unfortunately, very few of them are still in position for they have been knocked aside by motorbikes and tumbled into the stream by vandals lacking any appreciation of their historical importance.

A brake wheel was set in a pit to control the descent of the trams down the incline. Passing around the brake wheel was a continuous chain which was fastened to the trams on each line of rails. Grooves cut by the passage of the chain may be observed on certain stones still in place on the incline.

At Llanfoist Wharf is the old Wharfmaster's House and nearby is Hill's warehouse, locally known as 'The Boathouse'. This was once a bustling scene of industrial activity where the trams from Garnddyrys were unloaded and the iron products transferred to the waiting narrow boats to be taken to Newport Docks. Limestone and coal was transported in the other direction to Brecon. Michael Blackmore's splendid drawing depicts a scene from 'Rape of the Fair Country' when the people from Garnddyrys descended in the trams down the front of the Blorenge to pile into the narrowboats for their annual outing to Newport Fair.

Left: Llanfoist Wharf on the Brecknock & Abergavenny Canal. This drawing illustrates a scene from Alexander Cordell's novel 'Rape of the Fair Country,' when the ironworkers and their families piled into the narrowboats for their June outing to Newport Fair.

Above: *Entrance to the tunnel which passes beneath the canal at Llanfoist Wharf. It was constructed for pedestrian use and was no doubt used daily by the men who lived in Llanfoist and worked on the incline on the hillside above.*

Above: *This present day view from Llanelly Quarry of the west side of Clydach Gorge shows the development of tramroads and inclines during the period 1794 to 1830 and the Heads of the Valleys road constructed in the 1960's.*

Opposite: *A reconstruction of Llanelly Furnace based on a plan of c.1795 by J. Aran. This little charcoal-fired furnace was established in the 17th century by the Hanbury family of Pontypool. The nearby River Clydach supplied water power to drive a water-wheel operating a bellows which blasted air into the furnace.*

The wild and romantic Clydach Gorge, a century and a half ago would have been the scene of considerable industrial activity with nearly two thousand people; men, women and children employed in a variety of jobs associated with the production of iron. In about 1680 a charcoal-fired furnace was established in the lower part of the valley by the Hanbury family of Pontypool. It became known as the Llanelly Furnace and Captain John Hanbury is said to have built it, *'being engaged in the iron trade, like several of the Hanbury and Leigh family, and having already two furnaces at Pontypool.'* It was a well placed site, for wood was readily available to be converted into charcoal and there was also a strong supply of water for powering the bellows which provided the blast in the furnace. Michael Blackmore's reconstruction shows how the furnace was built against a bank so that it could be charged from above, and in front of the furnace can be seen a small casting house.

Sixteen sacks of charcoal were required to produce one ton of pig iron. An acre of woodland was only sufficient to supply enough charcoal to enable a mere three tons of iron to be produced. So it was not long before the hillsides in these valleys were bare of timber. The beech trees that can be seen in the upper part of the Clydach Gorge were planted as future fuel supplies for the Llanelly furnace, but when coal converted into coke took over as the fuel for the later ironworks, these beeches were fortunately left standing.

When the Ironworks and the Forge were put up for sale in 1813 the Forge property was described as follows:-

'Consisting of Two Hammers - Wheels and One Blowing Machine, Two Fineries, Three Hollow Fires, Capital Trevethick's Steam Engine for occasionally blowing the same. One Air - Chafery and Three Puddling and Balling Furnaces, Capacious Charcoal House, Smith's Shop, Warehouse, Agent's and 20 Workmen's Houses situated on the Railway, leading from the Canal. About half a mile from each.
It commands the same stream of water which works the machinery of the Furnace.
The neighbourhood abounds in Coppice Wood, and in the vicinity of the Tin Works occasions a constant demand for Charcoal Iron, for which this Works is in high repute.
It is held by lease from Capel Leigh, Esq., for a term of 81 years, from Midsummer, 1797, at a rent of £235 10s 0d per annum, and the whole of the works have been substantially rebuilt since that time.'

Clydach Ironworks were operated by the Hanburys of Pontypool until 1797, whn the widow of John Hanbury leased them to Edward Frere and Thomas Cooke, who also leased adjoining land from the Duke of Beaufort. Three years later they agreed to form a partnership with Edward and John Kendall of the Baufort works which resulted in 'The Clydach Ironworks Company'.

39

Edward Frere put thousands of pounds into the development of the works but further finance for the undertaking was always lacking. In 1803 Walter and John Powell joined the Company and introduced more capital. The partnership then went under the name of Frere, Cooke and Powell.

By 1809 Thomas Cooke had retired and John Powell had passed away leaving George Frere and a new partner John Jones in control of the works. George Frere was a hard worker and he had a high regard for his workers and generally treated them well. Many years after he had finished as manager of the works, he wrote a letter to the Rector of Llanelly Parish, recalling many of the old workmen that he had employed.

'John Williams, the Smith of whom I am justly proud, John Herbert, a Puddler, who turned over a new leaf for the better before I left. George Griffiths, the Smith, who had the habit of spending his money faster than he earned it, tho' he was a good hand at earning it too.'

George Frere obviously maintained a very good relationship with his workforce but it is recorded that *'he was swift to criticise and reprove his workmen for their personal conduct; he would confiscate and ruthlessly destroy the "fetchings" of beer which the men clubbed together to obtain from the inn, if he met one of them bringing the supply to the works. His riding whip was an "object of dread" to his workers if he returned from "the chase" to the works and found anything wrong there. He was himself a hard worker and an attentive manager; his ears ever open to the sound of the old forge hammer; and if the machinery was out of gear, he could be seen in the works, even in the depth of night, with little more than his night clothes on among his workmen.'*

The terrace of cottages that can be seen on the other side of the river is called Ynys-y-Garth and once housed key workers employed by the Clydach Iron Works Company. After being derelict for many years the cottages have recently been restored.

The method of working the inclines is described in a manuscript written by Thomas Jordan in 1909:-

'The materials...for the use of the ironworks, were brought down the hillsides by a series of inclines - each about three hundrd yards long, forming a zig-zag line down the mountainside. From the top of each incline to the foot of the next, was a level piece of ground forming a landing-place, where two men were stationed to pass the trams from one incline to the other. The inclines were self-acting, having the weight of the full trams going down drawing the empty ones up, and were controlled and regulated in their motion by a brake on a wheel over which an endless chain worked, and to which the trams were attached.'

The ironworks was put up for sale in 1833 and Messrs Powell took them over. By this time there were three blast furnaces, thirty-six coke ovens and a rolling mill. For the next twenty years the works did quite well and employed a large number of local people. But eventually the cost of bringing the raw materials down the tramroad and incline proved uneconomic. Also, the finished iron was of poor quality compared to that made by other ironworks and this resulted in a drop in demand. So by 1861 the works had ceased production.

There was a temporary revival in 1868, when Messrs Jayne and Sons made an attempt to develop a business in the manufacture of iron hurdles and gates etc... but it was not profitable and the works again closed down.

Above: *A present day view of the east side of Clydach Gorge showing the line of the Llamarch Railroad of 1795, various inclines and the route of the M.T. & A. Railway of 1862 which was built on Bailey's Tramroad of 1821.*

Opposite: *Clydach Ironworks as it might have appeared in the mid-1840's. Established here in about 1795 to take advantage of local supplies of iron ore, coal and limestone this works remained in production for about 65 years. The site was excavated in 1987 by Blaenau Gwent Borough Council and the impressive remains are now open to the public.*

Our next major task was to excavate the second furnace, which was in quite a bad state of repair and the stonework was very dodgy. We had to do a lot of rapid restoration work to hold the whole thing up. New lintels had to be installed into the rear passage and side entrances to the furnace to secure the vaulting and the overhead masonry. There is still a lot of work to be done on the cores of the furnace and we are hoping to build a lot of the blue furnace bricks back with modern engineering bricks.

The other area that we turned our attention to was the site of the casting house. We excavated a series of low walls, brick foundations and some large lumps of slag iron which were located centrally in the casting area.

It is difficult to work out the exact layout of the building because the walls are so fragmentary, but I think that one building probably spanned across both furnaces and that it was one very large casting house.

One of the most interesting things that we have found has been the pit of a water wheel - not the water wheel that we expected to find next to Furnace No 2 but the pit of another water wheel which was on the side of the charging house. This pit is quite a deep trough shaped feature. It is timber lined and there are still twelve timber floor boards in position. The vertical slots in the walls can still be seen and these probably held the wheel in place. This water wheel was almost certainly erected when Furnace No 1 was built and must have powered the blast for it.'

When asked where she came from, for she obviously hadn't grown up in Wales, Anne laughed and replied, 'I was born and bred in a market town in the wilds of Northumberland. Everyone here has been very friendly and welcoming. It is great to have such a hard working team as well and they have all developed a genuine interest in the project.'

IRONWORKS FROM NANTYGLO TO RHYMNEY

Brynmawr (Big Hill) at the top of the Clydach Gorge is the highest town in Wales and probably in Britain, for it is situated at an altitude of 1300 feet. Here winter always comes early and can be very prolonged.

Before 1800, Brynmawr as such did not exist for it was then just a group of scattered farms, making up a hamlet called Waun y Helegyn ('the field of Willows'). The people who lived here in this exposed place must have struggled hard to scrape a living from the bare hillsides. But all this changed in 1813 when the nearby Nantyglo furnaces were constructed and iron began to be produced. A township rapidly began to take shape here for the settlement was strategically placed between the Nantyglo furnaces and the Llangattock limestone quarries.

Many of the workers at the Clydach, Nantyglo and Beaufort ironworks made their homes at Brynmawr, but the industry of the town itself was the gathering of raw materials - iron ore, limestone and coal. It was said that the minerals which cropped out at the surface could in places be 'dug as potatoes from a garden.'

Women, married and single took their share in the work of gathering the iron ore and also loading and pushing trams in the levels driven into the hillsides. They would have taken their babies to work with them and children from an early age were employed to pick through the debris and look for nodules of ironstone.

Clydach Dingle on the northern outskirts of the town was the first scene of such activity. Here the ironstone was 'patched,' or the ground surface removed, in order to reach the ironstone strata. Iron-ore and blackband were collected and stacked in huge heaps which were burned to remove impurities before the minerals were sent to the furnaces.

A tramroad 8 miles in length was laid to the Llangattock quarries to bring limestone to the furnace at Nantyglo and there must have been a constant movement of horse drawn trams passing through Brynmawr.

Life in this town would have centred around the public house (there were once 82 in Brynmawr!) and the chapel. The first Brynmawr chapel was built in 1827 and by 1832 its membership, which at first was entirely Welsh, had reached 250, for a typical Welsh 'revival' had resulted in new members coming in at the rate of 25 a month.

Sickness and disease became a problem here for there was no town sewerage or water system and the inhabitants drew their water from numerous wells, some of which were seriously polluted. In 1847 there was a bad epidemic of cholera and an enquiry into the sewerage, water supply and sanitary conditions of the town in 1849 resulted in the Inspector's comment:

'It is scarcely within the power of the pen or pencil to convey to the apprehension of those who are dependent upon such sources of information, an adequate idea of the condition of the cottage tenements which constitute the town, as they presented themselves to my examination during the visit.'

As a result of the Inspector's comments a Board of Health was formed in 1851 and Brynmawr became a pioneer town in public health and administration. Conditions were gradually much improved although outbreaks of typhoid were still an occasional problem.

In 1789 a large tract of mountain land in the Parish of Aberystruth was leased by the Earl of Abergavenny to a partnership which was accordingly given the right *'to search for minerals, erect buildings, forges, and other works thereon.'* These partners were Thomas Hill of Stourbridge, in the county of Worcester, Thomas Hopkins of Rugely, Staffordshire and Benjamin Pratt of Great Whitley, Worcestershire. The yearly rent was £1,300 with an option to renew the lease at the end of the first seven years.

A further partnership was formed in July 1791 by Messrs. Harford, Partridge and Co., of Bristol with a view to establishing an ironworks on the site. It was agreed to erect two blast furnaces, casting houses, workmens' houses etc. as soon as possible.

Following a financial disagreement between the partners in 1795 the works remained idle for several years and they were described in the parish books as being 'empty'. In 1806 the first seven years on the lease came to an end and Messrs. Hill and Hopkins took out a new lease of minerals and royalties from Henry, Earl of Abergavenny, covering an area of 12,000 acres for a period of sixty-three years.

The partners Hill and Hopkins on 25th March 1811 agreed to sublet to Joseph Bailey and Matthew Wayne, an agent of the Cyfarthfa Ironworks at Merthyr Tydfil. They bought Nantyglo Ironworks from Thomas Hill and Samuel Hopkins for £8,000, which they borrowed from Morgan the Abergavenny banker. In a short time they developed the works into a prosperous business.

Ten years later, Matthew Wayne sold out his share of the works to Joseph Bailey and went off to develop another enterprise in the Dare Valley. Crawshay Bailey then took his place at Nantyglo. The Bailey brothers were the nephews of Richard Crawshay, being sons of his sister Susan who had married a Yorkshireman named Bailey. They quarrelled a great deal but rapidly developed the works by building a new forge and rolling mill. In 1825, they added an additional forge and a new plate mill was built in 1833. During this year the nearby Beaufort Ironworks was purchased and it was operated in conjunction with the Nantyglo works. Pig iron was brought from Beaufort to supply

Nantyglo, where the rolling mills were kept busy keeping up with a world wide demand for iron rails. Ten years later saw the addition of the Lion Mill and many extra buildings.

At the height of its prosperity the Nantyglo Ironworks employed 3,000 people and the site covered an area of 5,000 acres. Seven blast furnace produced 70,000 tons of iron a year and it was regarded as one of the most important ironworks in the world.

Five hundred and thirty houses stood on the five thousand acres of surface property belonging to the firm. There were twelve blast furnaces, seven at Nantyglo and five at Beaufort and with a complete range of forges, rolling mills and refineries. Twelve seams of coal were worked in the company collieries and under the property was an estimated quantity of 150 million tons of coal. Two veins provided the finest steam coal, while the ironstone was unlimited in quantity.

Two private railways connected the works with the Great Western and the London and North Western Railway systems, while a third, eight miles in length, brought limestone from the quarries of Llangattock. Above and below ground were 300 miles of tramroads. There were shipping wharves at Newport connected to the works by a private tramway, later replaced by the London and North Western Railway Company.

'I have been taken through the great Nant y Glo works at night, then at the zenith of their power and fame, and I knew both of the brothers, when in full vigour of life. Crawshay ruled the works at Nant y Glo and Joseph dispensing at times a lavish hospitality at Glanusk. My father was a contemporary and friend of them both, after meeting the elder brother at the Brecon and Abergavenny Canal meetings and occasionally over an evening rubber at Glanusk Park.

Both were individually men of strong character - great men we call them. Of course they had a bit of luck in finding the Black Band on the Beaufort hills, and probably in other ways, but their large fortunes were acquired mainly by their skill and industry, backed by proper capital to start with, and Nant y Glo and Beaufort works proved gold mines in their hands.'

John Lloyd 1906

Undoubtedly the area along the Heads of the Valleys saw the development of some of the greatest ironworks in Britain during the nineteenth century, and associated with them were the numerous collieries and towns with populations varying from 6,000 to 100,000 people.

When Joseph Bailey retired from the business he went to live at Glanusk Park near Crickhowell. In 1835 he became M.P. for Worcestershire. Crawshay retired in 1850, and he left his grand home at Nantyglo and moved down to the Usk Valley to take up residence at Llanfoist House. Turning to politics he became High Sheriff for Monmouth in 1850 and Member of Parliament for the Monmouth Borough from 1852 - 1868, when he was defeated by Sir John Ramsden, having previously fought five successful elections.

Crawshay left his nephews Richard and Henry Bailey to manage the Nantyglo and Beaufort works, but no doubt kept a very careful eye on them. The works were sold to the Nantyglo and Blaina Ironworks Co. in 1871 but then suffered from the general slump in the iron trade, caused mainly by the imports of cheap ore from Spain and the failure to convert to the new steelmaking process. Crawshay Bailey died on 9th Jan 1872 leaving an only son and heir, Crawshay Bailey the second (1821-87) who resided at Maindiff Court. In 1878 the Nantyglo and Blaina Ironworks company was finally wound up and its days of producing iron were finally over.

Development of the Nantyglo Ironworks

1795	First ironworks in Nantyglo is opened by Harford, Hill & Co.
1797c	Trosnant House built by Richard Harford.
1796	Works closes due to differences between the partners.
1802	Works is purchased by Joseph Harrison and re-opened.
1803	Works closes due to lack of capital.
1811	Joseph Bailey and Matthew Wayne purchase the works for £8,000.
1816	Construction of the two Round Towers by Joseph Bailey.
1820	Matthew Wayne leaves the partnership and goes to Aberdare where he establishes Gadlys Furnace. Joseph Bailey is joined by his brother Crawshay.
1822	A combination of workers at Nantyglo led by Josiah Evans and Harry Lewis defeat the local militia and reinforcements are called in to subdue the riots. Scots Greys were billeted above the stables of Ty Mawr for two weeks.
1825	Bailey's Tramroad is built between Govilon and Brynmawr. New furnaces and forge erected. The 'Black Band' is discovered.
1830	Seven furnaces now operate at Nantyglo.
1833	New plate mill is built.
1844	Lion Mill is opened and Nantyglo Ironworks is now one of the largest in the world.
1820	The Bailey Brothers purchase Trosnant House and the surrounding land and build Ty Mawr.
1830	Joseph Bailey retires to Glan Usk estate and enters politics.
1850	Crawshay Bailey retires to Llanfoist and also turns to politics. His nephews Richard and Henry now run the works.
1871	Nantyglo Ironworks is sold to the Nantyglo and Blaina Ironworks Company.
1872	Death of Crawshay Bailey on 9 January. He leaves an only son and heir Crawshay Bailey the Second, of Maindiff Court (1821 - 87).

Left: *Crawshay Bailey the famous ironmaster.*

TY MAWR AND THE ROUND TOWERS AT NANTYGLO

Trevor Rowson has lived in Nantyglo all his life and he is well respected by local people as an expert on the history of the area. He is able to describe from personal experience and with obvious feeling, the past industries of Nantyglo:-

"My father was a miner and I was born in Nantyglo at the time of the depression, when there was over 80% unemployment here. Consequently, my father and other local men opened their own levels and dug coal illegally. It was their way of supplying their families with coal, which was then essential, for all the cooking and washing had to be done on an open fire.

Looking further back, my grandfather came from Shropshire and he had not been here long before he made my grandmother pregnant. She was just thirteen years of age, and at that time it was considered a terrible sin. Well, he took fright, packed up his job, left Nantyglo and returned to Shropshire, leaving her in Limestone Road with her parents. She could not claim any assistance from the parish because she had given birth to an illegitimate child, so she was forced to work in the Tin Works at Nantyglo in order to maintain her child and she was employed there for several years.

Anyway, going back to myself, when I left school, I went straight into the pit at Abertillery. But I decided to study for a fireman's certificate, so I was put into a number of different collieries, studying various aspects of work. I went to Waun Llwyd, Garn Pit and several other mines. However, I never did get that certificate, but I enjoyed myself! I also worked in the Tin Works at Abertillery - so you can see I have a fairly thorough knowledge of employment in local industries."

Whilst Trevor had been talking we had been walking from the Round Towers car park towards the site of the famous ironmasters' house and at our feet now lay an excavated area with the foundations and cellars of the building well defined. Trevor pointed with both hands at the remains of the once grand building.

"This is *Ty Mawr* - 'the Great House,' which was the former home of Crawshay Bailey. As you can see it is a typical Georgian layout.

Here we are standing at the front of the mansion and you can see various rooms. Directly in front of where we are standing was an arched doorway and as you entered, immediately in front of you was a magnificent marble stairway.

If I can point out some of the rooms to you. This area would have been the drawing room...this would be the dining room...here was the closet area and various other rooms...whilst at the back of the mansion there were servants' quarters or the kitchen area.

In front of the mansion was a colonnade. It had a canopy with six iron pillars which were cast at the Nantyglo Iron Works. And here we can see the base of one of the stones which held the pillars supporting the canopy.

To our right there are a number of oval stones which were set against the mansion and these prevented the coach wheels from hitting the wall. As you can see from their shape, the wheels would skid off the stones.

Ty Mawr contrasted greatly with the workers' houses which were quite apalling. If we look across the valley we can see the remains of what was Bayliss's Row. These houses were constructed without windows on this side so that the occupiers would not be able to gaze out at the ironmasters' mansion.

In this small area we have discovered a toilet, and you can see a stone structure which connected with a tunnel which ran for over 33 metres down to the River Ebbw which, at that time, was nothing more than an open sewer.

The mansion itself was built on made-up ground and it provided the Baileys with a splendid southerly view while being sheltered from the sounds and smells of the works. It was quite a magnificent building.

In the area at the back of the house we can see where at one time there were three arches. There were two sets of stairs - one used by the servants and the other used by the tradesmen to bring their provisions down to the cellar areas, and over the top were the kitchen areas. Ajoining the mansion were a number of lean-to buildings - some of them were for lumber and various items used in the mansion.

Opposite: *A reconstruction of the Bailey brothers' estate showing their grand mansion known as Ty Mawr, the stable buildings and the two Round Towers. The house was built in about 1816 and it was approached through an avenue of trees and surrounded by large gardens. The servants lived in the old Trosnant House. It is said that the the higher of the two Round Towers could be reached through an underground passage leading from the house. The upper floor of this tower provided accomodation for James Wells and his family. He was a private secretary to the Bailey brothers.*

In front of the complex runs the 1828 tramroad from Beaufort to the Deep Pits in Nantyglo. The main stable block has changed very little in 150 years. Ty Mawr was demolished during the Second World War

49

Although Ty Mawr was built around 1816 there was an earlier house on the site and we can see its foundations in the corner adjacent to the mansion. This was built by Harford who was one of the first men to open the works here at Nantyglo, and it was then owned by Harford and Hill of Blaenafon.

It was quite an impressive house. The servants of Crawshay Bailey lived in it and there was a doorway on the side of Ty Mawr that the servants went through into the kitchen area."

Trevor then pointed across across the valley. "Over there you can see the first ironworks school built in 1828 by the Baileys. And at the time the inspector was Jeremiah Symonds who called at the school in 1841. There were 214 pupils on the books but there were only 11 in school that day. Out of the eleven, two of the children had limbs missing. But the headmaster assured the inspector that this was no problem for Crawshay Bailey had promised them employment at his works.

The small building over there was the salt house where the meat was cured and further in the yard the well is still there.

Ty mawr was occupied after the death of Crawshay Bailey by a series of managers. The last person to live in the house was Samuel Lancaster of Blaina. When he died in 1885, his body was taken from the house and put on a train to be buried at Highgate. Within a month there was a sale of furniture and effects from the house.

In 1900 it was still a substantial building and the miners decided that if they bought the property they could use it as a hospital. But a Dr. Bevan, who lived at Ty Meddig on the other side of the valley, went against the idea because he claimed it was too near the River Ebbw which was still an open sewer, so they abandoned the proposal. Ty Mawr was eventually destroyed during the Second World War."

We now turned our attention to the lower Round Tower on the north side of the property, and Trevor led the way inside.

"Because of the appaling social conditions and indeed working conditions, the Baileys feared for their safety and as there had been a number of riots at Nantyglo, particularly in 1816, they had this round tower built and kept it stocked with provisions.

The food was stored in the cellar and in the ground outside is a grid, for in order to keep the food reasonably fresh they had to have a circulation of air and that came through a heavy metal plate with holes in it covering a ventilation shaft.

This tower was kept provisioned at all times for fear of an uprising and we know for a fact that on at least five occasions the militia were billetted here.

You will notice that this tower has three storeys and much use of iron was made. Look at this ceiling support which is probably the only one of its kind in the world. It is made of slotted segments, all fitting into a central disc. Iron was probably used because it was much cheaper than timber.

We don't know the name of the architect for the Round Towers, but we can certainly assume that he must have had military experience. Take a look at the windows and the doors for example - which were designed for fortification.

After the death of Crawshay Bailey, the Round Towers in 1870 became residential. The people who then lived in them carried out modifications. For example, the floors were divided up into rooms for privacy. Children were actually born in here and it must have been absolutely appalling when you think that they had no light, no water or toilet facilities. People lived in here until just before 1945.

There was a difference in architecture between the northern and the southern towers for the latter one was a storey higher and the reason for this was that Crawshay's secretary, James Wells lived with his wife and two daughters on the top floor."

We ascended the hefty stone steps which are set into the outer wall and emerged into daylight on the roof of the tower. From the battlements we looked across the valley and Trevor continued. "As you can see from the top of this Round House, Bailey would have had a splendid view and he could have resisted any attack from his workers.

He could look straight onto the furnaces, the rolling mills and the refineries which were further up the valley. Over in the trees you can see Ty Meyrick, which was his surgeon's house, a man named Abraham Rowlands."

We made our way back down the curved stairway and Trevor paused at the doorway.

Left: *The Round Towers were built in 1816 (estimated date) to guard the Bailey estate and to provide refuge in times of trouble. It is said that Crawshay Bailey was a superstitious man and the towers were built round so that there were no corners where the devil could hide. At the present there is no access to the Round Towers but they can be seen from a nearby bridleway.*

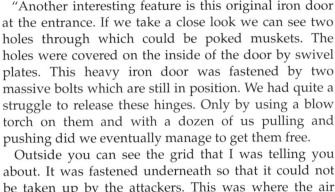

"Another interesting feature is this original iron door at the entrance. If we take a close look we can see two holes through which could be poked muskets. The holes were covered on the inside of the door by swivel plates. This heavy iron door was fastened by two massive bolts which are still in position. We had quite a struggle to release these hinges. Only by using a blow torch on them and with a dozen of us pulling and pushing did we eventually manage to get them free.

Outside you can see the grid that I was telling you about. It was fastened underneath so that it could not be taken up by the attackers. This was where the air passed through to provide a breeze through cellar to keep the food fresh. Just look at those walls, they are over five feet thick! At the entrance to the courtyard were two massive doors, one on the outside and one on the inside.

The upper Round Tower was blown during the First World War for its scrap iron. In the ground you can see a vent hole identical to the other one, but the iron grid is missing."

"What are your thoughts on the tale of the lost tunnel which is supposed to lead from the top tower to the cellar of the mansion?" I asked.

Trevor paused thoughtfully, before replying. "Well we don't really know, but we have had at least twelve elderly people on the site at different times who claimed to have been through the tunnel. We asked them to show us where the entrance was and it is significant that they all went to the same area. The only way that we are going to find it is by excavating the cellar of the tower.

Digging just outside the tower we have found a number of blocks which have been laid perfectly and it is possible that they were laid to cover the tunnel. The boys on the MSC scheme working under the direction of Doug Davies have done a very good job on the towers ensuring that they will be preserved for future generations.

The years 1831 and 1832, were a particularly bad time in Nantyglo. With a depression in the iron industry the workers were prepared to riot and we know that on at least five occasions the Redcoats were brought here and billeted in the top secion of the barns. It is interesting that these buildings were put up in two different periods of time. One section was built by the Harfords in 1794. You can see the join and the difference in the stonework that was used. The other building was constructed between 1816 and 1820. The iron water troughs were cast at the Nantyglo works.

I mentioned earlier about the use of iron for building purposes. Well, to hold the tiles on the roof they used iron bars, and copper nails were driven through the tiles and doubled around the bars. It is unique.

The estate was over 5,000 acres, which included the Ironworks. Over there you can see a small building which was the birthplace of Edmund Jones the Prophet. He was born there on April 1st 1702 and Crawshay Bailey used the cottage as a fowl house."

"What is that building with a green roof ? " i asked, pointing to the hillside.

"That used to be a house occupied by Tommy Evans, known locally as Tommy Donkey - not because he resembled a donkey, but because they shared the same I.Q.," Trevor replied with a chuckle.

"Is that a flag pole on the north tower?"

"Yes Blaenau Gwent Borough Council have donated a flag which will be flown from it."

"Ah, great, what is it?"

"Welsh Dragon - my mother-in-law," Trevor replied with a chuckle.

Please note: Restoration of the Round Towers was undertaken by a Community Programme funded by the Manpower Services Commission, sponsored and supervised by Gwent County Council. Additional funding was provided by the Wales Tourist Board and the Nantyglo and Blaina Town Council. The site is in private ownership and is part of a working farm. Access to the Round Towers and stables is no longer allowed, although it is possible to visit the site of Ty Mawr at any time.

BEAUFORT IRONWORKS

The Beaufort Ironworks began its life in 1780 when Edward Kendall from Derbyshire leased, from the Duke of Beaufort, all the mines and minerals in the parishes of Llanelly and Llangattock. His brother Jonathon joined him in 1798 and they erected two furnaces on farmland known as Gwaun Ebwy (the Glanyrafon area). The workers called the Ironworks 'Cendl' after the proprietors but it was oficially known as the Beaufort Ironworks.

They raised a weekly average of 300 tons of ore and converted it into pig iron, in a solid and square furnace standing 50 feet high and built into a steep hillside, which facilitated loading from above. The blast was provided by a large bellows driven by a water wheel. Initially the pig iron was sent to Glangrwyne Forge for refining but in due course a forge was built so that the pig iron could be worked into bar iron on the site. About 80 men were employed at the works and of these 30 or so worked around the furnace and casting house while the rest handled and transported the raw materials.

A third furnace was erected in 1804 to cope with the increasing demand for iron resulting from the Napoleonic Wars. Edward Kendall is said to have got into trouble for manufacturing bullets for the French during this period. By 1824 Furnace Number 4 had been built and a fifth one was erected in 1833 when the works was bought by the Bailey brothers of Nantyglo for £45,000

Edward Kendall lived at first in a small mansion which he built near the ironworks. The house was intially named Plas Gwaun Ebwy after the old hill farm that previously occupied the site, but it later became known as Beaufort House. Kendall was a widower and in 1801 he married a widow named Mrs Bevan who was one of the Gwynnes of Dderwen in Carmarthenshire. They settled at Danyparc, a large mansion near Llangattock in the Usk Valley. But their marriage only lasted six years for Edward suddenly died on March 7th 1807 at the aged 58, leaving his 15 year old son Edward to inherit the estates when he reached the age of 24.

Crawshay and Joseph Bailey bought the Beaufort works from Edward Kendall in 1833 and they worked them in conjunction with their Nantyglo Ironworks. Pig iron from Beaufort was rolled into rails at Nantyglo and Beaufort and like the works at Nantyglo it was connected with the canal by tramroad. The Beaufort Ironworks eventually closed in 1861.

EBBW VALE

Before 1790 Ebbw Vale was a hamlet known as Pen-y-Cae situated in a wooded valley beside the River Ebbw. It had a population of about 130 which was destined to rise within a hundred years to 12,000.

In 1791 Jeremiah Homfray bought some freehold farmland at Pen-y-Cae and erected a blast furnace. The pig iron produced was initially sold to other ironmasters in the neighbourhood who had already established puddling furnaces and mills but were not making sufficient pig iron to keep them going. In particular, Homfray supplied cast iron to Richard Crawshay of Cyfarthfa, the Llangrwyney Forge Company and Tredegar Ironworks. It was delivered by pannier-carrying teams of mules.

Homfray at this time obtained his ore and coal by 'patch' working and from an assortment of drifts and levels in the surrounding area. His limestone was conveyed by mules from Llanelly Quarries about 4 miles away.

In 1793 Homfray was joined by the Harfords whose capital enabled the business to expand. During the next three years the firm cast rails for the Trefil Tramway Company, whose tramway was constructed to convey limestone from the Trefil Quarries some 4 miles to the north of Ebbw Vale.

Homfray pulled out of his partnership with the Harfords in 1796 and the works continued to develop under the name of Harford, Partridge and Company. In 1818 they purchased the Sirhowy Ironworks and Collieries from Messrs Featherstone and Monkhouse. They developed the Ebbw Vale Works by erecting extensive puddling furnaces and bar plate mills and improvements were also made in smelting operations.

Cable iron was produced in 1825 in refinery furnaces with the use of coke saturated with a solution of common salt. Neilson in 1829 invented his process for

heating the blast before it entered the furnace and this was soon afterwards adopted by Harford and Partridge. The following year the first iron rails made in Wales were produced at Ebbw Vale and before long they were in tremendous demand. These included rails for the Stockton and Darlington Railway - the first railway in the world for passenger traffic. They were produced using the pre-heated blast technique pioneered by Neilson.

By 1834 the four blast furnaces at Ebbw Vale were each producing an average of 85 tons of pig iron per week and with the railway mania really taking hold, the demand for rails, for both home and export, grew considerably.

In 1844 the works was bought by Messrs. Darby of Coalbrookdale. The partners at this time were Abraham Darby, Henry Dickenson, Joseph Robinson, J. Tothill and Thomas Brown, the last named being the managing partner of the concern. The great-grandfather of Abraham Darby had founded the famous Coalbrookdale Ironworks in 1766 and the name of this family is still remembered in Ebbw Vale in 'Darby Crescent'.

Four years later the partnership took over the lease of the Victoria Ironworks and Collieries from Sir Benjamin Hall Bart; who in due course became Lord Llanover. These works which consisted of four blast furnaces, puddling mills etc., were built in 1836 by the Victoria Iron and Coal Company who subsequently failed, the lease reverting back to Sir Benjamin Hall.

George Parry, the works chemist was the first to successfully adopt the Cap and Cone on the blast furnaces for utilising the waste heat which escaped with the volume of flame issuing from the mouth of the furnace. This technique enabled the boilers supplying steam to the blast engines to be heated and also the blast before it entered the furnaces. It resulted in considerable economy in blast furnace operation.

In 1852 the Ebbw Vale Company bought the Abersychan Ironworks and Collieries from the New British Iron Company. They paid the trifling sum of £8,500 for these works which was more than covered by the stock of manufactured goods.

The Company further extended their holdings in 1855 with the purchase of an extensive iron tinplate works and collieries in Pontypool, comprising four blast furnaces, the Osborn Forge, Pontymoile Tinplate Works, the Lower Mills and Collieries where pig iron, corrugated sheet, tinplate, bar and sheet iron were manufactured.

In 1855 J.G. Martin of New Jersey, U.S.A. patented a process of refining iron which consisted of forcing a current of air or steam through the molten metal as it ran on the gutters which were perforated with small holes in the side and connected with the blast or steam. This patent was purchased outright by Messrs. Darby and exhaustive experiments were conducted with the object of decarbonising iron by forcing air or steam through the molten metal. It is interesting that experiments involving forcing air through molten metal with the object of converting it into steel were carried out by George Parry at Victoria three months prior to the first patent taken out by Sir Henry Bessemer. In 1856 Thomas Brown the managing partner in the Ebbw Vale Company applied for a licence to make Bessemer steel.

In 1861 Parry patented a process by which means he converted wrought or scrap iron into superior wrought iron or cast steel. It consisted of carbonising the scrap in a cupola furnace provided with special tuyeres. This patent process together with the Martin process, Sir Henry Bessemer purchased from the Ebbw Vale Company in 1866 for the sum of £30,000. Of this amount £10,000 went to George Parry.

In 1862 Thomas Brown retired from the management of the works and was succeeded by Abraham Darby as managing partner. The following year extensive new rail mills, bar and fishplate mills were erected adjoining the already existing 'Top Mills.' By this time there were about 100 puddling furnaces in Ebbw Vale and Victoria.

The Ebbw Vale Company now had at their huge works, 192 puddling furnaces, 99 heating furnaces, 1,200 workmen's cottages and also colliery leases comprising 7,500 acres of land.

In 1864 the whole concern was converted into a new company which was formed with a capital of £4,000,000 in shares of £50 each. The properties acquired consisted of the following:-
Ebbw Vale Ironworks, Collieries and Mines
Sirhowy Ironworks, Collieries and Mines.

Opposite: Ebbw Vale Steelworks was two and a half miles long and more than half of the working men of the town used to be employed in the works. Steel making came to an end in 1978, bringing to a close 200 years of iron and steel production in the western valley of Monmouthshire.

54

Victoria Ironworks, Collieries and Mines
Abersychan Ironworks, Collieries and Mines.
Pontypool Collieries, Ironworks, Mines and Tinplate Works
Abercarn Collieries.
Six Wharves at Newport, with hydraulic apparatus for discharging and loading cargoes.
The Haermatite and Coal Gales or Royalties in the Forest of Dean, County of Gloucester.
The Spathic Ore Mines (carbonate of iron) in the Brendon Hills, County of Somerset.

The whole concern was placed under the Managing Directorate of Abraham Darby and the General Management of William Adams. In 1865 Abraham Darby erected a new and powerful blast engine, on the south side of the Ebbw Vale blast furnaces which became known as the 'Darby'. The capacity of the blower was 27,100 cu ft. of air per minute.

In 1866 the Company was re-constructed when the Ebbw Vale Steel, Iron and Coal Company Limited was founded. The works was converted to steel production during the next two years and this enabled it to carry on into the twentieth century.

Spiegeleisen was first successfully and commercially produced at Ebbw Vale in 1879. The ore used was obtained from the Company's mines in the Brendon Hills, Somerset. The manganese and the Spiegel produced at this time being from ten to fifteen per cent. Prior to this date the Spiegel used in the Bessemer department was obtained from Germany via Rotterdam and Newport. Spiegel was also largely manufactured in 1872-3 at the Sirhowy and Abersychan furnaces.

In 1873 Abraham Darby retired from the Management of the works and was succeeded by Windsor Richards, who resigned the appointment two years later and Mr. J.F. Rowbotham took over as Manager. A new and powerful double cylinder blast engine was erected in 1879 on the north side of the blast furnaces at Ebbw Vale by Messrs. Darby of Coalbrookdale Ironworks.

During the 1920-30 depression the old Ebbw Vale Company was forced to close down its works which in 1936 were replaced by the huge modern Iron, Steel and Tinplate plant of Richard Thomas and Baldwin.

Over 6,000 men were employed in the Company's vast rolling mills, huge factories and steel sections. It was a very modern works with the first hot-strip mill in Europe and in 1947 the first electrolytic tinning line outside the U.S.A. was commissioned here.

By the 1950s there were four Bessemer converters each of 25 tons in production, but new blowing techniques involving a mixture of oxygen and steam were being introduced. Ebbw Vale by 1960 employed 9,000 people and was the largest completely integrated iron, steel sheet and tinplate works in Britain.

The works pioneered the L.D. oxygen method of steelmaking in Britain and was soon producing over a million tons of steel a year. The last Bessemer blow took place here in 1962.

In July 1967 the steel industry became state owned and at that time steel was the largest industry in Monmouthshire, providing employment to over 23,000 people who produced more than three million tons of steel a year. More than half of the working men of Ebbw Vale at this time were employed in the steelworks but a decade later in 1978 steel production came to an end here. Demolition of the works began in August 1979 and took eight years to complete. In 1986 work started in preparing the site for the 1992 National Garden Festival.

Right: Abraham Darby, Partner in Ebbw Vale Company, 1848. Managing Partner, 1861-1873.

Sirhowy and Tredegar
Ironworks

The first ironworks at Tredegar was started in about 1760 by a certain Mr Kettle who is said to have been a native of Shropshire. His single furnace was built of river stone and was about the size of an ordinary limekiln. An ingenious engine worked by a water wheel was used to blow the furnace instead of the old hand bellows and it enabled ten to twelve tons of iron to be produced weekly. His operations came to a close in 1778 when a local landowner, C.H. Burgh, granted a 40 year lease on land in this locality to a partnership comprising: Thomas Atkinson, William Borrow, John Sealy and Bolton Hudson. It allowed them, *'full liberty to build Furnaces, Forges, Mills, Engines and Storehouses.'*

Their coke fired furnace was the first one in Monmouthshire and it had an initial output of about four tons a week which was gradually increased to ten tons a week. However, the partnership collapsed in 1794 and Borrow the surviving member sought new partners. He was joined by a Bristol clergyman named Matthew Monkhouse and Richard Fothergill, a merchant banker from London who both wished to invest their money in an ironworks.

It became known as the Sirhowy Ironworks (sorwy meaning 'angry water') and by 1796 it was producing 1,820 tons of iron a year which at that time was an impressive amount. A second blast furnace was constructed the following year and a Boulton and Watt steam engine installed. This worked at 16 strokes a minute with a blowing cylinder 52 ins. in diameter.

In 1801 a third blast furnace was built and also during this year, production started at a new ironworks constructed half a mile down the valley at Uwchlaw-y-coed. It was named the Tredegar Ironworks after Tredegar House, the home of Sir Charles Morgan who was the father-in-law of Samuel Homfray. Morgan granted them a lease on the land he owned in Glyn Sirhowy extending from Brynmawr in the north to Bedwellty in the south on which they built their new ironworks. This was a new venture which had been set up in partnership with Samuel Homfray. In due course Tredegar Ironworks became the postal name of the new town which grew up around these ironworks.

An important development took place in 1805 when the Sirhowy Tramroad opened. Constructed under the Monmouthshire Canal Act of 1802, it was 32 kilometres long and joined the Sirhowy and Tredegar furnaces with the Pilgwenlly Wharves at Newport. It became one of the first passenger carrying railway lines in the world, and initially the tram loads of iron and coal were hauled by horses. Carriages with seats for fare paying passengers at this time was a unique idea.

The first section ran from Tredegar Ironworks to Nine Mile Point near Crosskeys, which took its name from the simple fact that it was 9 miles from Newport. From there the rails ran to the docks at Tredegar Wharf, Pilgwenlly, Newport. A one mile section of this railway ran through the grounds of Tredegar House (near Newport) and was constructed by the landowner Sir Charles Morgan who charged tolls with the result that it become known as the Golden Mile.

When the 1798 lease ran out in 1818 the Sirhowy Ironworks was sold to Harford & Company, a Quaker firm which operated the ironworks at Ebbw Vale. The pig iron produced at Sirhowy was used in their forge at Ebbw Vale. A boundary stone dated 1818 and displaying a letter 'S' can be seen near the Railway Hotel, and is one of several erected by Harford & Co., when they acquired the Sirhowy Ironworks.

In 1829 Samuel Homfray purchased a locomotive called 'Britannia' from Stepenson of 'Rocket' fame, and in due course it made its first journey from Tredegar to Newport. This historic event was described by the Monmouthshire Merlin in an issue dated Saturday 26 December 1829:

'It was confidently stated for some weeks past, that the Tredegar Iron Company at Tredegar Ironworks were to start a locomotive engine the day of the Cattle Show, on Thursday last, to bring the iron from the works to this port, a distance of 24 miles. The persons assembled at the Cattle Show (which was close to the tramroad) were looking anxiously for the steam engine, but it did not make an appearance. The engine did, however, start from the works early in the morning, but unfortunately, at one of the crossings in the tramroad, which was not long enough for the steam carriage, the wheels got out of the tram plates, which caused a detention of some hours, and on coming through Tredegar Park, the chimney

was carried away by a branch of a tree hanging over the tramroad and in consequence of these accidents it did not arrive at Newport till the evening.'

A few days later 'Britannia' hauled its first load of fifty-seven tons of iron along this route. Travelling at an average speed of six miles an hour it moved twice as fast as the tram horses and pulled double the load. Gradually the journeys were increased from two a week to a daily return trip with loads of up to seventy tons, including coal, timber and an occasional tram of lime or fireclay. Following on from the successful trial by Richard Trevethick at Merthyr, the 'Britannia' engine and the Sirhowy Tramroad can claim to have introduced the age of steam locomotion into Wales. The association of Stephenson's 'Britannia' with the locality is preserved in the name of a public house in Market Street, Tredegar - the Britannia Inn.

In the 1830s and 40s eight locomotives were built for the Sirhowy Tramroad, which included - 'Tredegar,' 'Jane,' 'Lord Rodney,' 'Lady Sail,' 'Charlotte' and one of the shunting engines on four wheels named 'Dispatch.' These were followed by two small locomotives for use on the narrow coal roads and then in 1852 the 'Bedwellty.' So eleven engines were built in Tredegar between 1822 and 1854. Daniel Gooch a young employee at Tredegar Ironworks went on to become Chief Engineer of the Great Western Railway.

In 1832 a rail connection was made between Sirhowy and Ebbw Vale when a 2.5 kilometre tunnel through the mountain was completed. Known as 'Harford's Tunnel' it was used to convey Sirhowy pig-iron to Ebbw Vale. Manufactured materials were also brought in the other direction and then transported along the Sirhowy Tramroad to Newport.

People on foot regularly used the tunnel as a short cut, particularly during bad weather when they had no desire to brave the elements by walking over the top of the hill to visit friends or relatives in the next valley. Above the entrance on the Sirhowy side was a stone, inscribed 'James Harford Tunnel 1832'. Unfortunately the entrances to the tunnel are now buried.

When, in 1844, the Ebbw Vale and Sirhowy Works were put up for sale at Bristol the tramroad-tunnel was listed as an outstanding feature of the undertakings.

Particular mention was made of the fact that it was walled and arched all the way through the mountain. It was still in use in the 1880's but by then it was only carrying occasional loads of goods to the Sirhowy Company Shop.

Right: *Sirhowy Ironworks was not only the first in Monmouthshire to be fuelled by coke but it was also one of the first ironworks in Wales to use steam power to blow its furnaces. The annual output in 1844 from the four furnaces was 7,000 tons of iron a year.*

In 1844 the Sirhowy and Ebbw Vale works were sold to Abraham Darby of Coalbrookvale. The inventory list for the Sirhowy Ironworks included: 'Five blast furnaces with hot-air apparatus to four of them, cast houses, Bridge Houses, Coke Yard, Two lime kilns, Clay Mill, worked by 22' waterwheel, three brick kilns and yards, 60" blowing engine, 52" blowing engine (both worked together with nine boilers), 30" winding engine, for raising lime and coal, four fineries and a winding engine, nearly new, not now in operation.'

The Sirhowy Ironworks closed down in 1882 having been in operation for 104 years. The site was unsuitable to make the change to steel production which was now in popular demand. Tredegar Ironworks on the other hand was able to convert to the new process the following year.

It has been claimed that the Tredegar Steelworks contained a network of the most powerful machinery in Britain and some of the most modern improvements of the time. There was an ordinary pair of blowing engines, made by Davey Brothers, Sheffield. The Bessemer had two ten ton convertors, with hydraulic tipping gear. There was also a 33 ins. cog mill with hydraulic lifting arrangements. The rails passed from the blooming mill, and then to the railbank, where they were straightened and drilled. They were made at 110 lbs to the yard, and about 60 ft. long. The longest rail rolled at these works was 120 ft.

In 1883 the output of the Tredegar Steel Works was considerable, but with the boom in the steel rail trade in 1884 it was virtually trebled. The climax in trade came in 1890 but this was followed by a steady decline until the works finally closed in 1895.

An attempt was made in 1835 to blow the furnaces at Tredegar Ironworks with hot blast, for previous to this date engines were blowing cold blast into the furnaces. Stoves were erected, and all the necessary fittings completed, but on the first night the scheme proved a failure and the tuyeres and pipes melted like lead. However the cause of the failure resulted in improvements which eventually proved successful.

Bedwellty House, is Gwent's best surviving example of an ironmaster's house. Originally it was the site of an old farmhouse called 'Coedcae y Cynghordy' which was purchased in 1800 by Samuel Homfray of Penydarren, one of the founders of the Tredegar Ironworks who desired a fine residence set in attractive parkland. The house which now stands on the site of the old farm was built by his son (also named Samuel) following his appointment as manager of the Tredegar Ironworks. He married the widowed daughter of Sir Charles Morgan and died without issue, so in due

course the house with its two entrance lodges and 26 acres of parkland was passed on to the Morgan family of Tredegar Park, Newport. It was reserved for occupation by managers of the Tredegar Iron and Coal Company until 1901. There are 20 spacious and beautifully fitted rooms and the outbuildings included stables, coach house and an ice house.

A marble tablet set into the wall at the southern entrance to Bedwellty Park commemorates the gift of Bedwellty House and its parkland to the town by Lord Tredegar in 1901.

Above: Bedwellty House, Tredegar, once the home of Samuel Homfray Jnr.

Left: The 'St David' was one of eleven locomotives built by the Tredegar Ironworks Company Engineer, Thomas Ellis. It is recorded that on 18 April 1848, the 'St David' hauled a train of 179 tons 19 cwt from Tredegar to Newport.

Right: *Tredegar Clock is a gaily painted clock tower which was erected in the mid-nineteenth century on the site of the old Tredegar Market Place. The aim was to commemorate the Duke of Wellington whose profile is shown on the massive base. The project was funded by the proceeds of a bazaar promoted in 1858 by Mrs. R. P. Davies, the wife of the manager of Tredegar Ironworks.*

The clock tower was manufactured by Charles Jordan, a Newport iron founder and was brought to Tredegar via the Sirhowy tramroad, which was an achievement in itself for the structure is 72 ft high and many tons in weight.

On 10 May 1958, a celebration was held to mark the centenary of the Town Clock. After a commemorative plaque was unveiled the crowd sang 'Happy Birthday' while the clock ticked away above their heads.

In
Memory of
WILLIAM
Son of
RICHARD and
CATHERINE GRIFFITHS,
of Tredegar Iron Works;
who died August 17th, 1849,
Aged 16½ Years
Also
RICHARD GRIFFITHS,
the above named,
died Septr. 10th 1849,
Aged 42 Years
fawr i fan.
'd och blau;

High on the hillside above Tredegar is Cefn Golau ('The Hill of Light') where a special cemetery was established after the dreaded disease of cholera hit the town in the autumn of 1832 and lasted until the spring of the following year. Healthy people who were walking in the streets in the morning would have the last tribute of respect paid to them by their friends in the evening. Large numbers of terror stricken inhabitants of Tredegar fled to the country to seek shelter, leaving their homes unguarded.

Above: *Cefn Golau cholera cemetery on the hillside above Tredegar.*

Right: *Remnants of Upper Furnace, Blaenrhymni, established in 1800, consisting of the hearth of a furnace can be seen in a field near the old Manager's House, just above the left bank of the River Rhymney. The house was built on leasehold land adjoining the furnace early in 1800, as a residence for the works Manager. Benjamin Hall lived here when he owned the works and subsequently RichardCunningham resided there. Nearby is a warehouse which bears the date 1802 above one of its doorways.*

In the December of 1849, cholera again broke out. The first victim was an Inland Revenue officer named T. Price, who resided at Charles Street, one of the healthiest locations in the town at that time. Before noon the same day, two stalwart and healthy men had fallen victim to the disease in the same street; and in less than a month there was scarcely a street in the town that was not affected.

The death rate rose so rapidly, and the symptoms were so terrible that the doctors became quite bewildered. Large numbers of people again fled to the country to avoid the scourge. A whole family residing in Charles Street was swept away in a day. The mother died about eleven in the morning and two children about four in the afternoon. The father assisted an aged lady, who acted as midwife in the locality, to place the remains of his beloved ones in coffins, as they were brought by the undertaker. Before ten that night the man was a corpse and as the following day dawned the aged lady also died.

When a funeral procession proceeded towards the cemetery, doors were closed, passers-by hurried out of sight, and very often barely sufficient numbers were found to convey the victims to their resting places. Camphor and various kinds of preventatives were worn by the majority of people day and night as an attempt at a prophylactic.

Ditches and drains were strewn with disinfectants, ordinary laws for preserving general health were enforced, sanitary improvements were insisted upon and every possible precaution was adopted. A cemetery was opened at Cefn Golau for burying those who fell victim to this terrible disease, and a circular was issued proclaiming of graveyards 'closed against those who died from cholera.'

It is a moving experience to walk around this windswept hillside cemetery on a misty day. Cefn Golau is a neglected and folorn place where leaning gravestones, inscribed mainly in Welsh provide a sad reminder of the days when good sanitation was unheard of by the local community who lived their lives surrounded by heaps of rotting rubbish, and all they had to drink was contaminated water.

RHYMNEY IRONWORKS

This was the most westerly of the Monmouthshire ironworks along the Heads of the Valleys and the settlement of Rhymney (Rhymni) takes its name from the river which rises in the moorland of Llangynidr. Its ancient name is Afon Eleirch - the Swan River, a descriptive and poetic name which was in use long before its water became polluted by industry.

Thomas Williams was one of the founders of the Old Furnace in Upper Rhymney and he was one of the first South Wales men to participate in the promotion of a new ironworks. Another partner was Richard Cunningham, who was also the manager. In 1803 Richard Crawshay of Cyfarthfa acquired the works and entered into a fresh partnership with Williams and Cunningham, his own son-in-law Benjamin Hall and Watkin George to form The Union Iron Works Co. with a capital of £29,000.

At this time the land belonged to the first Marquis of Bute through his marriage to the daughter and heiress of the second and last Viscount Windsor of Ireland, who had inherited this and all the Welsh estates including Cardiff Castle from his mother, the daughter and heir of Philip, seventh Earl of Pembroke.

An extensive network of rail communication, consisting of 20 miles of line, was developed by the Company connecting the two works and the limestone quarries.

The Monmouthshire Canal Act of 26 June 1802, which incorporated the famous Sirhowy Tramroad Company, also authorised a railway or tramroad of 4ft. 2 ins. gauge from Nantybwch to the Union Ironworks.

By 1815 the ironworks were also connected to the Bryn Oer (Brinore) Tramway, which linked Trefil Quarries by a well engineered route with the Brecon & Abergavenny Canal at Talybont.

Crawshay and Cunningham soon quarrelled and on the death of the former in 1810 the works passed on to Benjamin Hall Senior, who had married Crawshay's daughter. Their son was the Benjamin Hall after whom Big Ben is named. In 1823 the works was sold again, to a new company known as Foreman & Associates.

In 1825 an Act of Parliament gave consent to Crawshay and Joseph Bailey and Sir Charles Morgan *'for making and maintaining a tramroad from the northern extremity of a certain estate called Abertysswg in the parish of Bedwellty in the County of Monmouth to join the Sirhowy Tramroad at or near Pye Corner in the Parish of Bassaleg in the same County.'*

George Overton was engaged by the Rumney Tramroad Company to supervise its construction. It opened in 1826 and cost £48,000 to build. A group of Chartists travelled this route on their march to Newport in 1839.

The Bute Ironworks were, in 1835, erected on the Glamorgan side of the river on land belonging to the Marquis of Bute, and opposite to the works of the Union Company. The furnaces were constructed with massive stone facades introducing a new style of industrial architecture which was so unusual that drawings of them were hung in the Royal Academy. The style was described as Egyptian following a suggestion that it had been adapted from the most striking part of the ruins of Dandyra in Upper Egypt. Some years later the river which flowed past the works was turned to its present course to provide additional land for expansion.

A new company was formed in 1835 and constituted by deed of settlement in 1837 with a capital of £500,000 in 10,000 shares of £50 each. This company absorbed the Bute Ironworks from the Marquis of Bute and was known as the Rhymney Iron Company. An Act of Parliament was obtained giving the Company the right to build and support a church in the town. In addition it agreed to build a brewery and a new shop for the convenience of the local people.

In 1839 the Rhymney Brewery was started by Andrew Buchan primarily for ironworkers but it is of interest that in later times it was for the brewery rather than the iron that the town was known. The hobby horse trade mark depicting a man riding a barrel became a familiar sight in South Wales. Surviving pubs in Rhymney include 'The Puddlers Arms' and 'The Blast Furnace', providing memories of the industrial past of this valley.

The Rhymney Iron Company gained notoriety in the middle of the nineteenth century by the continuation of its 'Company Shop' - a system that had been abolished by the Anti-Truck Act of 1831. One of the six bells in the church of St. David in Ebbw Vale (built 1842-3) commemorates Andrew Buchan who at one time ran the Company Shop.

In 1864 the Rhymney Ironworks Company was conveying 180 tons of iron per week on the Bryn Oer Tramroad but by the following year it ceased operation.

The Bessemer process was adopted in Rhymney in 1867 and at this time 6 furnaces and 3 cupolas were being used for the manufacture of steel. The works enjoyed a twelve year period of prosperity but then closed down and was dismantled in 1890. One of the main reasons for the closure was the fact that there was no longer any local ironstone available and imported ore was proving too expensive to be economic. The Company then concentrated on coal production. Powell Duffryn took the Rhymney Iron Company over in 1921.

'While the coal trade grew and prospered, iron began to decay. Some of the older ironworks fell into disuse, among them the Rhymney works. By about 1890 its furnaces were blown out, and today only mounds of slag, thinly covered with rank grass, show where stood the once-thriving plant.'

T. Jones 1938.

Above:: *Butetown is a unique estate of ironworkers' cottages built between 1802 and 1804. The village was restored in 1970 and a small museum is contained in one of the dwellings.*

Butetown, situated 2 miles north-west of Rhymney is a unique estate of ironworkers' houses, designed and built by Richard Johnson, the manager of the Union Ironworks, between 1802 and 1804. Laid out in three parallel rows of terraces they formed a self-contained village situated some distance from the smell and smoke of the works, which was unusual for such times. It was Johnson's dream that this settlement, known originally as Trefnewydd (Newtown) would grow into a new town.

The central blocks of the terraces are a storey higher than the other houses and there are wide roads. Unfortunately the town was not completed due to the early death of Richard Johnson and it was named Butetown in honour of the Marquess of Bute who owned the land.

The village was restored during the 1970s by Mid Glamorgan County Council and Rhymney Valley District Council. In recent years a museum has been established in one of the houses.

IRON MAKING IN THE WYE VALLEY

It seems hard to believe now but at one time, iron, wire, brass, copper, tin-plate and paper were produced in the Wye Valley. Between the 16th and early 19th centuries this was a very important industrial area.

The beautiful Angidy Valley, above Tintern, in particular is a fascinating area to explore if you have an interest in industrial archaeology. From Pont y Saeson the Angidy brook falls 900 feet to the Wye and there are three small reservoirs in the valley known as the Upper, Middle and Lower Ponds which were all constructed to serve a series of industrial undertakings.

The first mention of this valley is in a charter granted to Tintern Abbey by William Marshall the Younger in 1223. It refers to the water of Angidy and the Abbey Mill of Angidy. At one time there were twelve dams, or dammed pools, numerous leats and no less than twelve water wheels here. It is significant that the first British water powered wire drawing works was sited in the Angidy Valley.

In 1565 Queen Elizabeth granted letters patent to William Humfrey and Christopher Schutz to *'search, dig and mine for calamine stone and also to make manure (manufacture) and work all kinds of battery works, cast works, and wire of latten, iron, steel and battery into and for all manner of plate and wire, or, otherwise needful and convenient for all manner of uses to their most benefit and profit.'* They formed a company called the Governors, Assistants, and Society of Minerals and Battery Works, and looked for a suitable site.

Humfrey and Schutz were sent to seek a suitable location for the proposed works. The Earl of Pembroke (one of the directors of the Society) was keen that they should set up the works in the grounds of Bristol Castle, but the water-power there was inadequate, so they inspected all 'the pleasant rivers on Severnside,' but found them all busily turning flour and cloth mills. So they crossed the Severn and found an ideal spot at Tintern in 1566.

They decided that the Angidy brook would be suitable for driving their hammers and machinery. Stones were taken from the Abbey to build houses for German workmen, and within two years wire was being sold to Bristol and Gloucester at £50.13.4 per ton. It was used mainly for making carding-combs for clothiers.

Humfrey and Schutz were dependent for the quality of their wire upon supplies of 'Osmond' iron. Initially iron was received from Monkswood and Pontypool but concern over the quality of the material led the Mineral and Battery Company to build their own furnace and forge at Tintern. They sublet their works to John Wheeler and Andrew Palmer who operated it until the lease expired in 1577. Three years later Sir Richard Marten took over the lease and in 1585 sublet to Richard Hanbury, who was a London goldsmith. He subsequently bought out the Company's ironworks at Monkswood which produced the iron that supplied the Tintern works.

Plentiful supplies of Osmond iron, which was now produced at the Upper Forge (situated immediately below the upper pond), enabled the business to quickly develop and Tintern wire became famous.

'Wire drawn so fine had never been produced in England before the installation of the Tintern wire mill...and it was highly regarded and spoken of in glowing terms. It was used to make many household goods such as pack needles, bird cages, mouse traps and curtain rods and they were distributed widely throughout the kingdom.'

H.R.Schubert

The history of the Angidy Ironworks is fascinating for it was managed by a long succession of people. Originally it was established as a concern independent of the wire-works, but both operations were worked with varying fortunes up to the end of the nineteenth century.

Marmaduke Rawdon of York came to Tintern in 1665 and wrote a fascinating description of the furnaces and ironworks:

'...the iron mills and the iron furnasses, where the iron is first smelted before it is beate by the mills into bars; which mill

works by the force of water. About halfe a mile higher up on the side of the hill are severall mills driven by water, where they draw wire from little iron bars into severall sieses... a curiosity worth seeing. The fire of the furnases where they smelt the iron is soe great, that, looking into the hole where the nosell of the bellows are, itt looks like the sun in a hot day at noone.'

He is describing the reduction of the iron into 'little barrs' - and from these were made fine wire. The furnace at this time was blown by a bellows but 110 years later the blast was introduced by compressed air by means of a cylinder and piston driven by a water wheel.

Charles Heath, writing in 1810 described how the wire was produced in the Angidy Valley during the 17th century:

'A large beam was erected across the building in which were affixed as many seats (in the form of large wood scales) as there were workmen employed, who were fastened in them by means of a girdle that went round their bodies. The men were placed opposite each other, while between them stood a piece of iron filled with holes of different bores for reducing the wire to the various sizes. When the iron to be worked was heated the beam was put in motion by means of a water wheel that moved it, with the workmen in their seats, regularly backwards and forwards, who, with a large pair of tongs, passed and repassed the iron through the holes till by force they reduced it to the sizes required. The motion was as regular as the pendulum of a clock; and if any of the men missed seizing the iron with his tongs he suffered a considerable shock in the return of the beam.'

From 1672 to 1751 the Foleys leased the Tintern Works and whether this lease included the wireworks or just the furnace and forges is not known. The directors of this firm were Paul and Philip Foley who were descendants of Richard Foley who had leased the Tintern Works in 1622

It is not clear whether the Angidy Furnace was in continuous production between 1672 and 1676, but the rate of output and the period that the furnace was maintained in blast indicates that it was worked intermittently. It is recorded that in 1672/73, over a period of 7 weeks, 1142 tons of iron were cast, even

though the furnace was idle for a period of five weeks. This gave an average yield of 18 tons 8 cwts per week. In 1675/6 the furnace was kept in blast for 61 weeks, during which time it produced 1034 tons of iron. It is recorded that in 1682 Chepstow exported 1,372 tons of iron.

Pig iron was sent to the Lower Forge at Tintern for refining into bar iron and it is recorded that during the period July 1693 - August 1694, 139 tons of iron were transported to the forge. During the same period a further 67 tons of Osmond iron were made at the Pont y Saeson Forge.

By 1698, 22 tons of cast iron were being produced in a week's operation. Charcoal was produced locally and the iron ore was transported from mines in the Forest of Dean, Porth Casseg and Portskewett. David Mushet who came here at the end of the eighteenth century commented:-

'When in full work, Tintern Abbey charcoal furnace, in Monmouthshire, made weekly from twenty-eight to thirty tons of charcoal forge pig iron, and consumed forty dozen sacks of charcoal, each dozen consisting of twelve sacks, and each sack consisting, or ought to have consisted of twelve bushels: so that sixteen sacks of charcoal were consumed in making one ton of pigs. The sack is assumed to weigh 180 lbs., which is very nearly the truth...

This was, I believe the first charcoal-furnace which in this country was blown with air compressed in iron cylinders, against which, for some years, a great prejudice was entertained on the part of the workmen, as being inferior to the air or blast obtained by means of bellows; so that when anything happened adverse to the furnace, the new blast was always in fault; but time overcame this silly prejudice, and the same keepers were fully sensible of their error when they came to make, with the new blast, nearly double the quantity of iron that had ever been reached by the old bellows.'

The two Tintern forges took most of the pig iron that was made here but substantial amounts were also transported by boat to forges in South Wales and the Midlands. William Morgan of Tredegar, for example, imported Tintern pig iron via the Wye and Severn to the mouth of the River Ebbw and Richard Hart of the Machen Forge probably used the same route.

Left: *The Angidy Ironworks was built in 1550 on the southern bank of the Angidy River. It was in operation for about 220 years. Excavated buildings on the site include the remains of the blast furnace which was originally 21 ft. in height. There was a storage pond further up stream from which water was conveyed in a wooden launder to power a water wheel, approximately 24 ft. in diameter. There was also a charcoal house, where charcoal was stored, a blowing house - where the twin bellows and later a set of cast iron cylinders were located. The cast house stood in front of the furnace and here the tapped molten iron would have run from the furnace into channels made in a bed of sand to be cast into pigs. In the background can be seen Crown Cottages, where ironworkers once resided.*

Records show that in 1717 the Angidy Furnace was producing 500 tons of pig iron and the two forges a joint 200 tons. The furnace consumed 600 trees a year, for it took 16 sacks of charcoal to make one ton of pig iron.

In 1730 the lease was taken up by Richard White, the son of George White, who had ironworks at the New Weir in Whitchurch. When Richard White died in 1752, he was succeeded by his nephew Edward Jordan of Shropshire. He was followed by Rowland Pytt Jnr. of Newland and Thomas Farmer who took over the lease in 1757.

On the death of Rowland Pytt in 1775, the works were leased to David Tanner of Monmouth, who also owned ironworks at Blaendare (near Pontypool), Redbrook and Lydbrook. Tanner employed 1,500 men at the Angidy Ironworks, which he operated for 24 years, finally going bankrupt.

In 1798 Robert Thompson purchased the works and built new mills further up the Angidy Valley, near Pont-y-Saeson. He lived in an impressive building at Tintern which had previously been owned by Richard White, (It is now the Royal George Hotel) and he also had a town house in Chepstow.

Charles Heath described his visit to Tintern in 1801:

'We left the great road at the village of Treleg, and passed through hollow and uncouth tracks, seldom attempted by any carriage but those of the natives. After a few specimens of pleasing recluse scenery, we enter a profound dell for several miles; a gurgling brook winding through the umbrageous cavity, which supplies a number of large ironworks above the village of Abbey Tintern; Mr. Thompson is the ostensible manager; the Duke of Beaufort the great proprietor. We inspected the principal furnace, and saw the ore, which is largely brought from that vast source at Furness in Lancashire, dissolved by the blasts of immense bellows, worked upon the modern construction of cylinder pumps. They have a method of separating the best qualities from the dross, by a water wheel and six hammers, from which they collect considerable quantities of pure metal, and the powder sells to the glass houses for their use. Lower down are various forges, for the purpose of striking the mutilated ore, into every requisite size and form of the broadest bars to the finest wires.'

Robert Thompson operated the works until his death on Christmas Day in 1820, at the age of 63 years. His tomb in St. Mary's Churchyard on Chapel Hill, above Tintern village, bears the epitaph:

'Robert Thompson Esq., the resident proprietor of the wireworks in this Parish, from the year 1798 to 1820'.

Following Thompson's death the works were put up for sale and a poster advertising 'Tintern Abbey Works' is of interest for it sings the praises of '... a stream of water; the River Wye, affording water carriage to and from all parts of England... unlimited supply of charcoal attached to the works and at command from other sources. Lancashire ore brought to the spot by water. Experienced workmen attached to their native spot are in abundance at reasonable wages.'

Messrs Briggs and Rowbotham then took over the works for a few years and they were succeeded by John Brown of Halifax, who closed the charcoal furnace in 1828, but operated the wireworks until 1846.

The Angidy furnace had always been fuelled with charcoal and now that coal was being widely used for smelting it was inevitable that this ironworks, which was not conveniently situated near a coal mine, should close.

During 1828, Prince Puckler Muskau, a German aristocrat travelled from Monmouth to Tintern in a post chaise and was probably one of the last people to describe the Angidy Ironworks in action:

'Leaving Monmouth, I took my way along the bank of the river to Chepstow. The country retains the same character, richly, deeply wooded and verdant; but in this part it is enlivened by numerous ironworks, whose fires gleam in red, blue and yellow flames, and blaze up through lofty chimneys, where they assume at times the form of huge, glowing towers, when the fire and smoke, pressed down by the weight of the atmosphere, are kept together in a compact, motionless mass. I alighted to see one of these works. It was not moved, as most are, by a steam engine, but by an immense water wheel, which again set in motion two or three smaller. This wheel had the power of eight horses and the whirling rapidity of its *revolutions, the frightful noise when it was first set going, the furnaces around vomiting fire, the red hot iron, and the half naked black figures brandishing hammers, and the ponderous instruments, and throwing around the red burning masses, formed an admirable representation of Vulcan's smithy.'*

John Hughes ran the iron and wireworks in 1850 and in 1871 Messrs Morrall & Stothart took over. The wireworks were operated for another twenty four years and it is of interest that in 1872, when the Wye Valley Railway was being planned, a decision was made to build a branch line to the wireworks. It involved the construction of a girder bridge over the river and this is still used by walkers making their way from Tintern up to the Devil's Pulpit near Offa's Dyke. The line opened in 1876 and it was hoped that this improvement in transport would help to increase trade at the wireworks.

In 1880 J. Griffiths & Co. took over the Lower wireworks and converted them to the manufacture of tinplate. (The Upper Wireworks which had been built in 1803 ceased production by 1876). They called their concern The Abbey, Tintern Wire and Tinplate Company and about 300 men were employed there. This firm ceased operating in 1895 and the works were taken over by the Abbey Tinplate Co., which closed down in 1901 and the plant was sold for £1,500.

It seems hard to believe now that Tintern was once an industrial village with roaring furnaces that employed no less than fifteen hundred people in work associated with the manufacture of pig iron and wire.

The final chapter in the history of the Angidy Ironworks relates to the period between April 1979 and May 1980, when the site was excavated as part of a Job Creation Scheme managed by Gwent County Council through the Manpower Services Commission, with grant aid from the Welsh Development Agency.

Archaeologist, John Pickin, who had directed the excavation of the Sirhowy Ironworks, a few years earlier, was put in charge of the project and he subsequently produced a detailed report on his findings.

Management of the site has since been carried out by Gwent County Council and Two information panels have been erected on the site to provide a detailed explanation of its operation. A leaflet describing the site is available at the Old Station (April- October).

Coed Ithel Furnace

The remains of this Wye Valley furnace (ST 527027) can be seen on the left hand side of the A466 (which was built in 1803), when approaching Llandogo. Situated on a hillside about 30 ft. above a stream the remains date from the 17th century and consist of a 20 ft. high section of furnace with evidence of a waterwheel pit behind it. It was originally owned by Sir Richard Catchmay who lived in nearby Catchmay Court. The site is very overgrown and access rather difficult. There are traces of a watercourse running due west and north.

W.H. Thomas described the furnace in 1839:

'At Coed Ithel, part of the interior of a furnace still stands, its walls vitified and impenetrably hard as in the day of its activity and use, but where the flame of commerce was once lit, a stately tree has taken root, spreading its branches far and wide.'

The furnace has been excavated and it was found to be typical of a mid-seventeenth century furnace. Between 1672 and 1676 it had an average weekly output of 18 tons and iron ore from the Forest of Dean was used. It was probably in production until about 1717. Coed Ithel means the 'Wood of Ithel' who was the son of Arthrwys a King of Morganwg in the 6th century.

Trellech Furnace

Situated in Woolpitch Wood, near the village of Trellech (ST 487048) is the remains of a very overgrown charcoal furnace with a tree growing out of it. The best time to see this site is in winter. The furnace dates from about 1650 and is square in shape - 26 ft. square at the base and at a height of 10 ft. from the ground it is about 20 ft. square. A nearby stream would have provided power for driving a waterwheel.

Whitebrook Wireworks

In 1606 the Mineral and Battery Company built an additional wire-works four miles from the works at Tintern on land leased from the Earl of Pembroke in a valley which is now known as Whitebrook. The works was constructed to take surplus orders which the Tintern works could not handle. Driven by water power it was operated until 1770.

Paper mills were later erected on the site of the former wireworks between 1770 and 1847 to take advantage of the exceptional softness and purity of the water from the White Brook which was ideal for use in the manufacture of paper. The mills were called Upper Fernside, Lower Fernside, Sunnyside, Clearwater, Wye Valley and The Glyn. Banknote paper was produced here and it was shipped on barges to Bristol. The last mill ceased operating in 1890 and the ponds were later used for rearing trout.

Redbrook

In 1692 there was a copper works at Redbrook with 16 furnaces. The copper was mined in Cornwall, shipped to Chepstow and brought up the Wye to Redbrook by the famous Wye 'trows'. Copper smelting ceased here before the end of the eighteenth century when iron became the new fashionable industry.

The Redbrook furnaces and two iron forges at Lydbrook (Gloucestershire) were leased in 1762 to Richard Reynolds, John Partridge (Senior) and John Partridge (Junior) for 21 years.

During 1771 the site was sold to was sold to Messrs Townsend & Wood who erected a tinplate works which in later years produced the thinnest hot rolled steel sheet in the world, used for hermetically sealing tins of food, drugs and tobacco. These sheets were called 'taggers' and were rolled in the hot state in packs down to as thin as 0.0025 ins, a seemingly impossible task for a hand mill.

A Boulton and Watt steam engine was installed here in 1798 and worked until 1944 when it was replaced with electrical driven plant.

In 1799 Archdeacon William Coxe travelled through the Wye Valley during his famous tour of Monmouthshire and wrote:

'About two miles from Monmouth a small stream called Redbrook - where some iron and tin works give animation of the romantic scenery'.

In 1898 the works was taken over by the Redbrook Tinplate Co. and the adjoining Wye Valley Railway served the site with its one freight train per day and the continuing trade no doubt helped to prolong the life of the railway for goods traffic.

The works operated until December 1961 when competition from the big strip mills proved too great and it was forced to close down, throwing 150 men out of work, after operating for just a decade short of 200 years. It was the last tinplate works in Britain where tinplate was still made by the traditional hand method.

OTHER MONMOUTHSHIRE FURNACES AND FORGES

Abercarn

Abercarn can claim the distinction of being among the three oldest centres of the Welsh iron trade. Situated on the main stream of the River Ebbw the first furnace was built by Edmund Roberts and purchased some time before 1597 by Richard Hanbury. It closed down in about 1748. Two years later John Griffiths, who had been manager for Capel Hanbury at Pontypool built a new iron-works at Abercarn, but he only remained there seven years, after which he disposed of the business.

The next ironmasters of whom there is any record were the Glovers of Birmingham, who for a quarter of a century, carried out a lucrative trade at Abercarn. They acquired the works in 1782 and supplied Anthony Bacon of Cyfarthfa with 800 tons of pig iron per year.

In 1808 the works was sold to Richard Crawshay and was described by Britton and Bayley as the *'extensive ironworks of Abercarn: the late property of Samuel Glover, Esq., consist of a foundery; a tilting and fuming mill; an Osmond forge; a wire mill, capable of drawing a hundred bundles of wire per week; a forge with shingling and finishing rollers, which will shingle seventy tons per week; and a rolling mill, that will convert sixty tons per week of half-blooms into bar iron. The Monmouthshire canal passes through the works, which are supplied with coals from a colliery one mile and a half distant, brought down a tramroad to the canal.'*

Abercarn was once a manorial estate and just over a century ago the lord of the manor was Sir Benjamin Hall, who for some years lived with his wife (later Lord and Lady Llanover) at Abercarn House before they moved to the village of Llanover.

The location of the Abercarn Ironworks has been regarded as someting of a mystery until quite recently. Three local amateur historians, Len Burland, Foster Frowen and Lionel Milsom, who specialise in the industrial past of the Ebbw and Sirhowy valleys of Gwent, had been interested for a number of years by legend, heresay and various mentions in local writings concerning Abercarn Ironworks. All traces of that ironworks were believed to have disappeared under the march of progress. However these three men in 1993 made a remarkable discovery which they described as follows:-

'Local records gave us no real information about the Abercarn Ironworks, or its location, but they gave us early dates. John Lloyd's *Old South Wales Ironworks* tells us that Abercarn Ironworks was buying pig iron from Hirwaun Ironworks in 1783; a paper in Birmingham Reference Library includes Abercarn in a list of charcoal blast furnaces which had declined blowing, dated 1st Jan. 1788; that date is corroborated by Coxe in his *Tours in Monmouthshire*, who lists Abercarn as having a charcoal furnace - not used.

Like many before us we felt that there was no hope of finding any remains of a two hundred year old blast furnace, or any other parts of the ironworks, which we assumed were lost under the extensive Abercarn Tinplate Works and later Abercarn Colliery.

One Friday evening in the autumn of 1993 we had finished a walk around Abercarn and stopped to lean on a wall behind a small supermarket, looking over its back garden. Our eyes were drawn to a stone-built structure at the back of the garden. We immediately jumped to the conclusion that its shape, apparent age, and proximity to water in the Nant Gwyddon, made it something worth further investigation.

Permission was sought to enter that garden the following Sunday morning, and many more mornings over the next two years. The clearance of rubbish revealed a recess in the stone wall, and a long cast iron beam, which we now know was the upper part of the casting arch of a blast furnace, with its top lintel. The chance find was as simple as that. There were no pre-conceived ideas, just a look over a wall and the eye of faith proved us correct.

Two years of work followed, leading to the clearance of more of the casting arch, revealing three cast iron lintels. The dangerous nature of the ground stopped us researching the hearth. We also managed to find a way of wriggling under the bridge-arch, which was also in a

dangerous and partly collapsed state. That arch is unusual by its length of 8.92 metres (29 feet), if not unique.

Many libraries and reference sections have been visited and we have found enough original documents, an inventory and an early map to give us a full picture of the setting up of a company in 1750 by four partners; that the furnace was working in 1753 and that it was blown out in 1788, but that the other parts of Abercarn Ironworks continued in use, relying on pig iron brought into the works from other ironworks, even by boat to Newport from as far away as Lancashire (a trade that existed at Abercarn as early as the 1760's).

We were able to use this original material to supply Mike Blackmore with enough information to make a reconstruction of how Abercarn Blast Furnace would have looked in the mid/late 18th Century.

We know that the furnace, bridge arch and bridge house were one stone built streucture which a contempory document lists as 67 feet by 28 feet, measurements that exist today. There was a water wheel supplied by two water sources, a leat and a launder, depending on water supplies at different tomes of the year. Bellows were used under the bridge arch. There was a large charcoal hose. There were four calcining kilns.

What remains of the furnace make Abercarn the most complete charcoal blast furnace in Gwent or Glamorgan.'

Blaendare

In 1785 David Tanner of Monmouth established coal furnaces at Blaendare, near Pontypool. The cold blast was derived from a bellows driven by a water wheel which was operated by an overflow from the Glyn Ponds. In 1799 he went bankrupt and left the country. The Blaendare furnaces were purchased by John Barnaby, a Herefordshire man, for £10,000. In 1804 he sold the works to Capel Leigh Hanbury in order to concentrate on coal mining. The pig iron produced at the Blaendare furnaces was taken by packhorse to the Park Forge and the old Osborn Forge where it was converted into bars.

Blaina

This works was founded in 1823 when George Jones of Wolverhampton leased lands and mineral rights in the parish of Aberystruth. In 1827 he formed a partnership with John Barker. They constructed three furnaces and operated the works at great profit for several years until the partnership was dissolved in 1835.

In 1839 the works was sold to Thomas Brown of Blaina and John Russell of Pontymister. The three furnaces produced 2,400 tons in 1825 and 4,905 tons in 1830. A fourth furnace was built in 1839 and it is recorded that the works had a weekly output of 240 tons of bars and iron rails. The works was later sold to Messrs Levick and Simpson who expanded the operation rapidly and in due course purchased the Coalbrook Vale works as well.

The Blaina Works was later acquired by Crawshay Bailey and leased to Messrs Levick and Simpson. After Crawshay Bailey died the Nantyglo and Blaina Ironworks Company was formed with John Richardson as director.

British Ironworks

This ironworks was originally known as the Abersychan Ironworks and it was established in 1826 by Shears, Small and Taylor on land leased from the Wentsland estate for the purpose of manufacturing merchant bars. It was taken over in 1829 by the new British Iron Company which consisted of two to three thousand people who bought shares at £50 each. No profit was made by the Company for the first eleven years.

A complete village was constructed for all the ironworkers who were housed in rows bearing names such as Monmouth Row, Elizabeth View, East View, Norfolk Row, York Place, John's Row, Dublin Row, King's Parade, Queen's Parade and Mount Pleasant. They all had cast iron window frames made in the works. The foremen or overmen lived in a larger house at the end of each row.

In the 1830s the pig iron was all produced by cold blast and the average weekly output of a furnace was from 70 to 80 tons. There were no coke ovens and all the coke used was made in the open air from large coal, the loss in coking amounting to about 43 per cent.

Iron rails were first made at these works in 1840 and both rails and bars in various proportions continued to be made until 1850, when the production of bars ceased, except for home use, and rails became the sole product. The first rails were all made from cold blast iron.

In 1848, hot air was introduced into the blast furnaces, and, although coal was used in the stoves - the waste gases not yet being utilised - the heated air soon proved to be an important factor in both the saving of fuel and increasing the output, which soon reached 120 to 130 tons per furnace weekly.

Open coking was next abandoned and coke ovens substituted, by which a further saving of 30 per cent was made in the quantity of coal used to produce a ton of coke.

Prior to the opening of the Monmouthshire Railway from Newport to Pontypool in 1851, and subsequently from Pontypool to Blaenavon in 1853, the transit of raw materials and iron was by canal. The head or terminus was at Pontnewynydd, which was later linked to the works by tramroad. Iron ore and other material brought up by boat from Newport was conveyed to the works in horsedrawn trams, and in the same manner the bar iron and rails were taken down to the canal head and conveyed by boat to Newport for shipment.

In January, 1852 the works and collieries held by the British Iron Company under lease from the Lords of the manor of Wentsland and Bryngwyn, were acquired by the Ebbw Vale Company. The British Iron Company had gone bankrupt in 1851 after spending £400,000; the works was sold for just £8,500. Such a purchase sum for the buildings, plant and machinery, workmen's cottages, and stocks of material, barely represented one-fifth of the value of the concern. It was said at the time that the stock of ironstone on the pit banks alone, represented a sum equivalent to the amount of the purchase money.

In 1857 the works was sold to Messrs Weston & Grice, who remodelled the plant and machinery and confined their operation to the manufacture of nuts, bolts and fish-plates.

Subsequently this firm acquired the Cwmbran Collieries and blast furnaces, which then belonged to John Lawrence, and operated the works under the title of 'The Patent Nut and Bolt Company, Limited.' The firm was later merged into the big combine known as 'Guest, Keene & Nettlefolds, Limited'.

Within a few years following a drop in prices the works was sold to the Ebbw Vale Company for £8,500 and they at once proceeded to construct the necessary railroads for connecting the works with the Monmouthshire line, which had just been opened. To make a junction with the main line, which was considerably below the level of the works, the railway company constructed an incline plane from Talywaun to a point on the line called Twynyfrwd, about mid-way between Varteg and Abersychan.

This incline was worked by a stationary engine, and a special rate of 3d per ton plus the tolls was charged by the railway company on all traffic conveyed on it. Later on, the upper level line from Pontypool to Talywaun and Brynmawr was constructed and the incline abandoned.

Various improvements, costing large sums of money were carried out at the works by the Ebbw Vale Company. The most important being the application to the blast furnaces of the cup and cone. This arrangement enabled the waste gases to be collected and applied to the heating of the hot air stoves and blast engine boilers, for which purpose coal had previously been used.

Not only did this method result in a large saving in fuel, but it also increased production which rose to 200 tons, and finally, just before the closure of the works, in 1876, to about 250 tons per furnace, per week.

When the demand for iron rails declined in about 1868 - 70 due to the popularity of steel, the British Ironworks went into decline and closed in 1876 putting a large number of people out of work. Soon afterwards the works were completely dismantled, the buildings, plant and machinery, being broken up and sold.

A three-storey Cornish type engine house, built in 1845, survives on the site. It was built to house a Cornish Beam Engine which, powered by steam, was used to drain the Company's mines. The location of the furnaces is recognised by the remains of masonry and evidence of ironmaking on the ground - iron ore, coal, coke, limestone and a large lump of charge (containing these ingredients) can also be seen.

Caerleon Tinplate Works

In 1749 John Griffiths who had been manager to Capel Hanbury at Abercarn, left after a disagreement and took over a forge site on the Ponthir Road at Caerleon in partnership with Samuel Watkins. Two years later John Griffiths sold his share to Lewis Davis of Hatton Garden, London and went to America, where he established ironworks at a place called Kingsbury.

When Archdeacon Coxe made his tour of Monmouthshire in 1800, the works were owned by John Butler. They were then capable of producing annually 14,000 to 20,000 boxes of tin plates. Iron bars, rods etc were also made. The machinery of the mill is described as being 'wholly of iron' with a large water-wheel and two fly-wheels. The water providing the power was conveyed along a channel leading from the Afon Llwyd.

Horse drawn trams brought the finished products along the tram road to the old wharf at Caerleon Bridge. Here the boxes of plates were transferred to a boat named the 'Caerleon Man'. Handling the boxes was extremely heavy work; great skill and strength was required to carry them from the trams to the hold of the boat. The vessel was worked by means of long oars down the River Usk to the Severn and then sailed to Bristol.

In 1818 Richard Fothergill who was a partner in the ironworks at Sirhowy took a lease of the works here and a great period of prosperity ensued. He lived in a house called the Back-hall but died in 1821. He was succeeded by his second son Thomas, who carried on the works until his death in 1858.

Rowland Fothergill, brother of Thomas then took over. In about 1870 the works were occupied by the Moggridges of Blackwood and later by David Grey of Maesteg. After being closed for some time they were then taken over by Richards & Hopkins who brought them up to date.

The Caerleon & English Works Ltd, as it was then called, was wound up in March 1912 but the following month it started up again under the name Caerleon Tinplate Works. In 1914 the works was registered as the Caerleon Works Ltd. and had a prosperous period during the First World War. It eventually closed in 1940.

Coalbrookvale Ironworks

This works was started in 1820 by George Brewer who was related to the Darbys of Coalbrook Dale and this explains the name Coalbrookvale. He died in 1845 and his son Tom Llewellyn Brewer took over as ironmaster. In 1825 the two furnaces had a yearly output of 5,200 tons and by 1839 there were 3 furnaces which had a weekly output of 500 tons.

Cwmbran Ironworks

These works were established in the 1840s by F.J. Blewitt of Llantarnam Abbey and were acquired in the 1870's by Patent Nut and Bolt Company of Smethwick, near Birmingham. The managing director was Arthur Keen who later formed a partnership with Guest and Nettlefolds which became a famous name for iron and steel in South Wales. They continued in production until 1923 when the mills were modified to roll steel sheet. Near Cwmbran used to be a canalside inn called the Forge Hammer and the nearby forge boasted the second largest steam hammer in the world.

Cwmffrwdoer Furnace

In 1825 when a site was being cleared for the foundations of the Pentwyn furnaces, which were being built by the Hunt brothers, the remains of an early smelting furnace were revealed.

It was the site of a blast furnace erected by Richard Hanbury in 1579. He built furnaces here and at Trosnant to make use of the Blaenafon ore. Three years previously he had acquired large tracts of woodland between the Ebbw and the Usk, which included iron mines belonging to the Earl of Pembroke. In addition, he took possession of all the woods within ten miles of Tintern and also the best mines in the County for extracting the Osmond. By 1580 he had built additional furnaces at Abercarn and Monkswood.

Glyn Trosnant Furnace

This was named after the Trosnant Brook and situated in the Glyn Valley at a location called 'Old Furnace'. It operated prior to 1578 until possibly as late as 1850, but later the old forge was partially demolished during the Civil War and iron was manufactured here until 1831.

Two large ponds supplied the works with a good quantity of water and the extensive woods in the valley provided ample means of making charcoal.

In the early 1970s it was still possible to see a half section of the stone furnace and remains of stone buildings nearby. The site was excavated in 1973 by Pontypool Local History Society who discovered part of the charging platform and evidence of the early blast furnace. Soon afterwards the site was covered with tipped material prior to the construction of a garage on the site.

Govilon Forge

The name Govilon is derived from 'gofailion' meaning forges. John Harris was the proprietor of the Govilon Forge at the end of the eighteenth and the beginning of the nineteenth century. There would have been smiths working here at open coal-fired hearths, manufacturing small metal objects such as knifes, scythes, wire and nails. They worked from rods of wrought iron. The forge was subsequently taken over by a Mr. Matthews, who in about 1850 sold it to James Charles Hill who made a fortune here and retired to a house named The Brooks that he built near Abergavenny. In later years this house was demolished and Nevill Hall built on the site by the Marquis of Abergavenny. After the death of James Hill the Govilon works went into decline.

Llangrwyne Forge

Walter Watkins of Dan-y-Graig in Llanelly is generally accredited with the founding of the Ebbw Vale iron industry. In 1789 Walter Watkins erected an iron works at Pen y Cae, Ebbw Vale in partnership with Jeremiah Homfray and Charles Cracroft of Crickhowell. They smelted iron ore for working into bars and merchant iron at Watkins's Llangrwyne Forge. Two years later their company was dissolved with Watkins and Cracroft assigning their shares to Homfray who agreed to supply Watkins with pig iron and iron plates at an agreed price. Situated in the Grwyne brook which provided power, there was a good supply of wood for charcoal in the neighbourhood. The Forge probably dates from the same period as the Llanelly Forge.

Walter Watkins who had the estate of Dan y Graig through his wife (daughter and co-heir of Thomas Morgan), was the first pioneer of iron industry in this district and worked the forge. He was High Sheriff for Breconshire in 1775 and died in 1799, being buried with his wife in Llanelly Church, at the age of 63.

In 1792 when the Brecknock and Abergavenny Canal was built Walter Watkins was anxious to have a bridge made across the Usk at Llangrwyne by the Canal Company to enable a tramroad to connect with Ebbw Vale and other ironworks and get his pig iron to the forges.

The bridge was built in 1794 and just completed when melting snow in February 1795 flooded the Usk and destroyed the bridge and the land embankments on either side. The builder had been under contract to maintain the bridge for three years so the Canal Company required him to reinstate the bridge at his own expense. He refused to do so and his non-liability was upheld by a Herefordshire jury at the trial. It was declared that this great flood and disaster was an Act of God, the consequences of which he was in no way responsible. The bridge was never rebuilt and the Llangrwyne Company were still obliged to cross the Usk to their works by a dangerous ford.

Machen Forge and Tinplate Works

The earliest forge was established here in 1569 and by the time of the Napoleonic Wars it was producing impressive quantities of iron. It was situated near the river which provided the power; local woodland supplied the fuel, and Iron ore and limestone were readily available in the locality. In 1826 the forge changed over to tinplate manufacture. The works had its own tramway to connect it with the Rhymney Railway and the bed of this tramway still exists, being used today as a lane. In 1842 the works consisted of two water and one rolling mills, scouring pots, scale house, tin house, work house and a shearing machine.

In 1852 the Machen Forge was known as the 'Machen Iron and Tinplate Company.' By 1886 the works fell into disuse and some of the buildings were demolished soon after this date. By 1910 little was left on the site for the stones had been mostly removed for building purposes.

Monkswood Ironworks

Known in Welsh as Capel-y-coed-y-mynach this works

was at one time associated with the estate of Tintern Abbey - from the original endowment by Walter de Clare. The monks had a grange or hermitage in the wood just north of the road. It is recorded that in 1562 Richard Hanbury constructed a furnace and two forges or hammer mills at Monkswood, where the line of the old mill stream could at one time be seen near the lane called Rumble Street - named, no doubt from the jangling of iron as it was carried away on pack horses. Richard Hanbury was the subject of various law suits in consequence of his claiming the right of pre-emption of woods in this locality for the burning of charcoal to provide fuel for the manufacture of iron.

In 1564 a company called the Mineral and Battery Works were established here, by whom the works was let on lease in 1574 to John Wheeler and Andrew Palmer.

There was a furnace near the Stop-gate, Monkswood on the Usk Road, worked by the Berthin brook. There were also two forges or hammer mills here and the iron produced was of special quality known as Osmond iron.

Osbaston Forge, Monmouth
A furnace existed on the north side of Monmouth during the latter part of the 16th century. It was destroyed by rioters in 1588. A new forge was erected in 1684 and during the next 180 years it changed hands many times. In 1869 it was converted to tin plate production and finally closed in 1886.

Park Forge, Pontypool
On the east bank of the river at the bottom of Trosnant, Pontypool a furnace and forge was erected in 1575 by John Truve and from 1580 - 90 it was owned by Thomas Fermor. It is shown on the Ordnance Survey map of Monmouthshire published in 1833 but it would appear that it ceased production in 1831.

Pentwyn
An ironworks was erected here by the Hunt brothers in 1825.

Pont Gwaithyrhaearn (The Bridge Ironworks)
In the 18th century (1738-9) two Frenchmen from Brittany fled from their native country during the war that raged between England, France and Spain, in the early part of the reign of George the Second. They landed in England and travelled to Wales where they erected a furnace at Pontygwaith in about 1739 and began smelting ironstone here. Their furnace was charcoal fired and blown with a hand bellows. The smelted iron was turned into saucepans, kettles and small agricultural implements. The furnace ceased operations when the two Bretons returned to their homeland in about 1747.

The old farm of Pont Gwaithyrhaearn stands near the site and it was probably there before the furnace was built. The furnace produced an average of 120 tons of iron a year which was sold mainly as pig iron. The ironstone to supply the furnace came from Rhos-y-Mwyn, Pen-y-Bryn and Bryn Oer.

Pontnewynydd Forge
This was sometimes called the 'Little Forge' and was situated below the river bridge at Pontnewynydd and it was probably as old as the Town and Park forges. The famous 'Osmond' or 'Osborn' iron was made here from the time of Queen Elizabeth to the reign of Charles the Second. It was considered to be the most malleable and ductile iron then known. The wireworks at Tintern used this iron and also similar iron produced at Monkswood near Usk. Ore for making the Osborn iron was obtained from Elgam Mountain to the north of Blaenavon.

Ponthir Tinplate Works
This was built in 1747 by J. Jenkins (senior) in partnership with a certain Mr. Conway. In 1818 the ownership passed to Richard Fothergill who ran the works until 1858, when his brother Rowland Fothergill took over.

Pontnewydd Tinplate Works
In 1802 a tinplate works opened at Pontnewydd using the Afon Lwyd for power. A second works opened here in 1806.

Pontnewynydd Ironworks
Pontnewynydd owes its origin to the ironworks which were started in 1837 by John Lawrence and William Morgan (of Llanfoist).

In about 1845, William Williams of Beaufort, who had kept the Bailey Brothers' Company Shop, acquired these works and manufactured bars and rails. He failed on the collapse of the Monmouth & Glamorgan Bank in 1851. He also owned the Golynos Works and resided at Snatchwood House.

A Mr. Henley of London then took over the works, which he converted into wire mills. But before long they were idle and after many years were acquired by another company for the manufacture of tin-plate and sheet-iron.

Pontyfelin Tin Works

This works was erected in 1703 by Major Hanbury on the banks of the Afon Lwyd at Pontyfelin near New Inn. It consisted of two tin-mills and a small charcoal forge.

Pontymister Ironworks

This works was in operation from 1810 on land bounded by Ochrwyth, the River Ebbw and Pontymister Bridge. It had a rolling mill which produced 40 tons of bar iron per week. In 1814 the works was put up for sale after its manager John Thomas went bankrupt.

Pont-y-Moel Tin Works

This works was sometimes referred to as 'The Old Plating Mill' and it was built in 1745 for the manufacture of tin-plates at 'Old Estate Yard', Pontymoile. A tram road was constructed in about 1825 running from Pont-y-Moel Tin Works along the side of the river to the Park Forge, then on to the Lower Forge and the New Forge. It was later extended to Osborn Forge and this involved two bridge crossings of the Afon Lwyd.

At the upper end of Cwmynyscoy a tunnel was made to connect the Blaendare furnaces with Pont-y-Moel and also one was dug under Sowhill to connect Cwm Glyn with Osborn Forge.

Trostre Forge

A small forge was once in operation on the bank of the River Usk situated at a convenient spot to obtain power from the full flow of the river. It was once the property of the Fludyer family and was operated between 1790 - 1800 and leased by Harvey, Wason & Company. Bar iron was manufactured here which was sent by land to Newbridge-on-Usk and then by boat down the Usk to Newport for shipment to Bristol.

John Lloyd writing in 1906 observed that:

'Tradition relates that this was a fatal spot to the passing fish, especially those descending the river, as a huge chamber, with iron bars at the lower end, was used for passing the river water through when the Forge Wheel was not working; and that in spring time a great slaughter of foul fish, and later of the descending salmon fry, took place, and that this fish trap was, in fact incidentally a source of profit to the occupiers of the Forge and Mill.

The high flood of 11th February 1795, reached a record point here, some two feet above the doorway of the mill, and a stone niche shows still the level, and in which a recording brass tablet had been placed by Messrs Harvey, Wason & Co. The tablet is not there now, but I have seen it; and anxious to restore and preserve historical marks like this, I offered - but in vain - £5 to its present possessor to allow me to have it to refix in its proper place. Monmouthshire men should see that this is done.

The Forge pound, as it is called, above the weir forms, I think, the largest pool on the Usk, and the deepest, being probably larger than Newton pool at Brecon, Llanddety pool at Buckland, or the Bridge pool at Crickhowell.'

Welsh ironmasters used to meet occasionally at the Three Salmons Hotel in Usk where they dined on Usk salmon. It was considered that the fish was at its best when caught after twelve hours in the fresh water. In 1782 a salmon of 68 lbs was caught near here.

Town Forge

This very early forge was situated just below the Town Bridge in Pontypool on the town side of the river. Here the pig iron from Old Furnace was converted into wrought iron having been delivered here on the backs of Spanish mules.

Both Town Forge and Park Forge were fairly close to the Park mansion and the constant annoyance from smoke and the deafening sound of the hammer caused Capel Hanbury to have them dismantled in 1831.

Grove Cottage was built from the stone of the Town Forge. It is recorded that in 1883 some remains of the works were still to be seen, including the boundary of the pond, and the wooden shafts of a water wheel.

Varteg Forge

This small forge was built in 1802 by Thomas Hill on the eastern bank of the Afon Lwyd at Cwmavon above the present road bridge. It was in production by November 1804 and was driven by water power. There is a large arch keystone dated 1804 set into a wall at SO 269065 and the furnace was sited at SO 264056. Nearby an incline was constructed - leading down to the Blaenafon Railroad

Varteg Forge probably refined iron from the Blaenafon furnaces. By 1819 the works were leased to Fawcett, Whitehouse, Hunt & Co. The partnership was dissolved in late 1825 and the Hills sold out to Kenricks & Co.

Perched on the hillside above the site of the Forge is a row of twelve cottages built in 1804 appropriately known as Forge Row (SO 270064). Restored in recent years they were originally built to house the Varteg Forge ironworkers. Apart from Stack Square, Blaenafon, built in 1792, this is now the only surviving example of housing from the first phase of the Industrial Revolution in Gwent.

Victoria Ironworks

In 1837 the Victoria Ironworks came to the village of Coed yr Anglwydd - The Lord's Wood, just south of Ebbw Vale. Matthew Wayne was engaged to erect a works here and the foundation stone was laid on May 24 1837 by Sir Thomas Lethbridge. The land was held under a lease from Sir Benjamin Hall, afterwards Lord Llanover. A village of 200 houses was built and the streets were named after the landowner, Benjamin Hall and his wife Augusta.

The Victoria Iron and Coal Company took its name in honour of the Princess Victoria, Duchess of Kent, who came to the throne the following year. By 1848 the Company was in financial difficulties and the lease reverted to Sir Benjamin Hall to then be taken over by Abraham Darby for the Ebbw Vale Company.

The works at this time consisted of four blast furnaces, a puddling mill and other machinery. In 1894, 14 men were being employed for shifts of 12 hours at each furnace which turned out between 600 and 800 tons of pig iron per week. Steam lifts raised the raw materials to the tops of the furnaces.

A new American style furnace was built and put into action in 1904 - known as No.3 Victoria. It was the largest, being 75 ft. in height, 18m ft. 6 ins. diameter of the bosh and hearth diameter 11 ft.

In 1740 Monmouthshire only had 2 blast furnaces in operation, producing 900 tons of pig iron. By 1909 there were 14 at work with an output of 324,261 tons, but the old ironworks had closed down and the main centres of the iron and steel industry were at Blaenavon, Blaina, Cwmbran, Ebbw Vale, Panteg, Pontypool, Risca, Tredegar and Victoria.

Many of the ironworks in South Wales tried to change to steel production, but because of the necessity of haematite ore, which had to be brought in from other parts of Britain or abroad, it was uneconomical to transport it inland from the ports.

Today the only steelworks in Gwent is at Llanwern to the east of Newport. Standing on a site of 2,800 acres its construction represented the largest ever civil engineering project in the United Kingdom. This three mile long works opened in October 1962 with the only fully automated strip mill in the country.

CHRONOLOGY OF IMPORTANT EVENTS IN THE MONMOUTHSHIRE IRON INDUSTRY

1425c David & Ieuan Graunt begin smelting iron at Pontymoel.

1526 Monkswood Ironworks is established by Richard Hanbury.

1565 Ironworks is established at Pontypool by Richard Hanbury.

1566 Britain's first water powered wire-drawing mill is established at Tintern.

1568 Brass is made for the first time in Britain at Tintern.

1600 First furnace is established at Blaenafon.

1645 The first iron forge in America is built by emigrants from Pontypool at Lynn, Massachusetts.

1650c Woolpitch Wood Furnace is constructed at Trellech.

1660 Coed Ithel Furnace is constructed near Llandogo.

1680 Llanelly Forge is built by John Hanbury.

1684 Llanelly Furnace is in production.

1695c The rolling mill is invented at Pontypool.

1703 First commercial production of tinplate in Britain is carried out at Pontypool.

1709 Abraham Darby uses coke to replace charcoal for the first time in Shropshire.

1730 The technique for Japanning iron is invented in Pontypool.

1735 Abraham Darby succeeds in using coal converted into coke as a fuel for his Coalbrookdale works in Shropshire.

1738 Pont Gwaithyrhaearn Furnace is established.

1740 A coke burning furnace is erected by Capel Hanbury in Pontypool.

174? Abercarn Ironworks is established.

1750 A new Ironworks is built at Abercarn by John Griffiths.

1753 John Wilkinson builds the first coke-fired blast furnace in Wales at Bersham in Clwyd.

1757 Coke is introduced to South Wales at the Hirwaun Ironworks.

1776 A steam blowing engine is used by John Wilkinson in the blast furnace process at Bersham in Clwyd.

1778 Sirhowy Ironworks, the first coke-fired blast furnace in Monmouthshire is established. In that year it produces 1,930 tons of iron.

1779 Clydach Ironworks is established by Edward and John Kendall.

1780 Beaufort Ironworks is established.

1782 Abercarn Ironworks is purchased by the Glovers of Birmingham.

1783 Henry Cort patents his grooved roller technique for making malleable iron into bars.

1785 Blaendare Furnace is established by David Tanner.
1786 Henry Cort patents his method of refining iron by puddling.

1789 Blaenafon Ironworks is established by Thomas Hill and Thomas Hopkins.

1790 Furnaces are erected at Ebbw Vale.
Final year of production of iron using charcoal at Llanelly Furnace, Clydach.

1790c Trostre Forge is established on bank of River Usk.

1791 Nantyglo Ironworks is established by Harford, Partridge & Co.
Jeremiah Homfray erects the first blast furnace at Ebbw Vale.

1793 Furnaces are constructed at Clydach.

1795 Nantyglo Ironworks is established.

1796 Newport to Pontnewynydd section of the Monmouthshire Canal is opened.

1796 Production of iron at Clydach is 1,660 tons.

1798 Beaufort Ironworks begins production.

1800 The Clydach Ironworks Company is formed.

1801 Tredegar Ironworks is started.

1802 Varteg Forge is established by Thomas Hill.

1803 The Union Ironworks Co is formed at Rhymney.

1804 Blaendare Ironworks is purchased by Capel Hanbury.

1808 Abercarn Ironworks is purchased by Richard Crawshay for Benjamin Hall.

1810 Pontymister Ironworks is established.

1815 First ironworks school in Wales is established at Blaenafon by Sarah Hopkins.

1818 Samuel Baldwin Rogers uses iron instead of steel bottoms for the furnaces at Nantyglo and doubles the output of each furnace.

1820 Coalbrookvale Ironworks is started by George Brewer.

1823 Blaina Ironworks is established by George Jones and John Barker.

1825 Pentwyn Ironworks is erected by the Hunt brothers.
Cable iron is made at Ebbw Vale in Refinery furnaces with the use of coke saturated with a solution of common salt.

1827 Abersychan Ironworks is established

1829 James Nielson invents the blast process.
First iron rails in Wales are made at Ebbw Vale for the Stockton & Darlington line.

1830 British Ironworks Company is formed.

1833 Bailey brothers purchase the Beaufort Ironworks.

1834	Discovery of Black Band iron ore near Nantyglo.
1835	Bute Ironworks at Rhymney is established.
1837	Furnaces are set up at Pontnewynydd by John Lawrence and William Morgan. Victoria Ironworks is established at Coed yr Anglwydd.
1843	Cwmbran Ironworks is established by F.J. Blewitt of Llantarnam Abbey.
1844	Ebbw Vale Ironworks is bought by Messrs Darby of Coalbrookvale.
1850	George Parry at Ebbw Vale Ironworks introduces a 'Bell & Hopper' to close the top of the blast furnace. Crawshay Bailey retires to Llanfoist.
1851	Pontnewynydd Ironworks is purchased by W.T. Henley and converted into wire mills.
1852	British Ironworks (Abersychan) is acquired by the Ebbw Vale Company.
1855	J.G. Martin patents a process for refining iron by forcing a current of air or steam through the molten metal.
1856	Ebbw Vale Works adopts the Bessemer process soon after its discovery.
1861	Beginning of depression in local iron trade. Beaufort Ironworks closes. Final production of iron at Clydach Ironworks. George Parry at Ebbw Vale patents a process to convert scrap iron into wrought iron or cast steel by carbonising it in a cupola furnace.
1866	Ebbw Vale Steel, Iron & Coal Company founded. Nantyglo and Blaina Ironworks Company is formed.
1867	Bessemer process is adopted at Rhymney Ironworks. Blaina and Coalbrookvale Ironworks closes.
1868	Spanish ore begins to be imported to South Wales.
1871	Nantyglo Ironworks is sold to the Nantyglo & Blaina Ironworks Co.
1872	Crawshay Bailey dies.
1873	Strike along the iron belt for increased wages (it lasts 3 months). Beaufort Ironworks closes.
1873c	Haematite ore ceases to be used in Monmouthshire ironworks.
1874	Nantyglo Ironworks closes down.
1876	British Ironworks is closed and dismantled.
1878	Sidney Gilchrist Thomas devises a process to remove phosphorous from steel. Nantyglo and Blaina Ironworks Company is wound up.
1879	Spiegeleisen is first commercially produced at Ebbw Vale.
1882	Sirhowy Ironworks closes down.
1883	Tredegar Ironworks converts to steel making.
1888	Ebbw Vale Works is converted to steel production.
1890	Rhymney Ironworks closes and is dismantled.
1895	Tredegar Steelworks closes down.
1936	Steel and Tinplate plant of Richard Thomas & Baldwin is opened at Ebbw Vale.
1938	Ebbw Vale strip mill begins production.
1947	First electrolytic tinning line outside USA is commissioned at Ebbw Vale.
1951	The steel industry is nationalised.
1955	Ebbw Vale becomes the largest single site tinplate production unit in Europe.
1959	The government agrees to loan Messrs. Richard Thomas & Baldwin the sum of £70,000,000 to finance the construction of a new steelworks at Llanwern.
1960	Ebbw Vale pioneers the L.D. oxygen method of making steel in Britain. Ebbw Vale is producing over a million tons of steel per year.
1962	Llanwern Steelworks begins production with a steel-making capacity of 1,400,000 ingot tons a year and with the rolling mill plant capable of producing 3,500,000 tons a year.
1967	The steel industry becomes state owned and steel is now the largest industry in Monmouthshire, providing employment for over 23,000 people.
1978	Steel making comes to an end at Ebbw Vale.

Right:: *A typical scene on the Brecknock & Abergavenny Canal.*

THE CANAL AGE

The canals of Wales were all constructed in one decade from 1790 to 1800 and it was no easy task, for the steep hills and deep valleys were difficult terrain in which to build a canal system. Most of the labourers who built these canals came from farms and villages in the area, but a good many also came from other parts of Wales such as Cardiganshire and Carmarthenshire. They were known as navigators or 'navvies' and their work was hard and dangerous, with no compensation for injury or loss of life.

Following excavation, the canal bed had to be lined with a watertight seal which was created with a mixture of loam and clay. This was 'puddled' and spread over the bottom and sides of the cut to a depth of 18 in. to 3 ft. Sometimes cattle or sheep were driven along the bed of the canal to assist the puddling process.

Many thousands of men were employed and the impact that such a large workforce had on small rural communities was notorious, with incidents of theft, rape and murder quite common.

During this period the average earnings for the canal navigators varied from 1s to 1s 6d a day, while skilled tradesmen such as the carpenters who made the lock gates could earn as much as 11s a week.

The main effect of the canals was to accelerate the progress of the Industrial Revolution but as working concerns they had quite a short life. The railways quickly took over as the prime system of transport and by 1900 the waterways were carrying very little traffic at all.

THE MONMOUTHSHIRE CANAL

Construction of the Monmouthshire Canal began in 1792 for the purpose of transporting the mineral traffic of the hills to Newport. The main promoters were Sir Charles Morgan of Tredegar, William Esdaile the London banker, Josiah Wedgewood, the Ist Duke of Beaufort and Thomas Hill the ironmaster. The initial estimate of the cost of the canal construction was £108,000, but the final figure was nearer £220,000. It was built in two arms which joined about a mile above Newport. The western branch ascends the Ebbw Valley via Risca and Abercarn to Crumlin, while the eastern branch follows a fairly straight course northwards past Malpas and Pontnewydd to Pontypool where it joined up with the Brecknock & Abergavenny Canal.

The construction of these two arms involved a combined rise of 793 feet and, the associated construction of 74 locks, 2 tunnels and 3 aequducts. By comparison the Brecknock & Abergavenny Canal only needed 6 locks, 1 aqueduct and a 375 yard tunnel.

By 1812 the towns of Brecon and Newport were connected by a complete system of inland navigation.

Canal building certainly created a considerable amount of employment in those days, but it was the canals themselves that were to lead to real economic growth during the Industrial Revolution of the nineteenth century.

CRUMLIN ARM (Western Branch)

This 11 mile branch of the Monmouthshire Canal ran from Crumlin in the Western Valley through to Rogerstone and then eastwards to meet the Eastern Valley branch at Crindau, just outside Newport.

The construction engineer was Thomas Dadford Jnr., who already had considerable experience in canal building, having previously assisted his father in the construction of the Glamorganshire Canal.

In 1791 the *British Chronicle* of Hereford commented that the proposed canal to Crumlin *'would open up an easy and commodious communication with divers iron works, limestone quarries, woods of timber trees, and collieries.'*

Between Crindau and Crumlin, Thomas Dadford found it necessary to construct 32 locks. He built 5 at Allt yr Yn and 14 at Cefn (Rogerstone).

Thomas Dadford Jnr. is buried at Llanarth near Abergavenny and the inscription on his gravestone reads:

```
IHS
In memory of
Thomas Dadford
Late of Crickhowell in the
County of Brecknock
ENGINEER
Who departed this life
April the 2nd, 1801
Aged 40 years.
```

FOURTEEN LOCKS, ROGERSTONE

The flight of fourteen locks at Rogerstone is not unique among the canals of England and Wales but it is certainly a remarkable feat of late 18th century engineering achievement. It had to rise 168 feet within half-a-mile and a staircase of locks was the only answer to this problem. However, an additional consideration was that an enormous quantity of water would obviously be needed to fill every lock each time a barge passed through. To fill a single lock took no less than 40,000 gallons of water.

Thomas Dadford decided to conserve water by building a series of balancing ponds alongside the fourteen locks. This meant that the water from the top lock could be drained into the first balancing pond and re-used in the next lock below - and so on all the way down the staircase. Well at least that was the theory, but the re-cycling of water never proved as efficient in practice, particularly in the summer when there were frequent water shortages.

But Dadford's design certainly helped to ensure that there was a constant level of water through the locks and the header ponds also provided passing places for the barges. A special 'sea lock' was also built to provide a passing place. It has two shelves of differing depths which meant that two boats, one ascending and the other descending could pass each other here. The heavier of the two (usually the descending craft) could pass over onto the lower shelf and the lighter boat would go onto the higher one.

Half way down the flight of locks can still be seen the lock keeper's cottage (Pensarn Cottage). He was responsible for keeping the locks and towpath in good order and for reporting any leaks on the lock gates or any dangers of subsidence in the canal banks.

When the canal was first built, Squire William Phillips who lived at Risca House, laid a wager that he would jump his horse over a lock. Sadly the animal slipped and tumbled into the lock while Squre Phillips fractured his skull. However, being a hardy gentleman, he survived but had a metal plate in his head for the rest of his life.

Located at the top ponds is the 14 Locks Canal Visitor Centre and Picnic Site which was established in 1975 by Gwent County Council and Newport Borough Council. Inside is a fascinating exhibition which tells the story of the Monmouthshire Canal. The Centre is open daily between April and October, from 10.00 am to 5.30 pm. It is generally closed on Tuesdays andWednesdays.

A half-mile waymarked trail starting from the centre leads you around a fascinating and complex system of locks, ponds and channels. The 14 Locks are designated as an Ancient Monument.

Beyond Rogerstone the bargees had a further 19 locks to negotiate before they reached the end of the canal at Crumlin. It involved a total ascent from Crindau of 358 feet. The building of this canal was no mean task but amazingly, it was completed in just three years.

Opposite:: The Monmouthsire Canal at Allt yr Yn. There were 32 locks on this western arm of the canal between Crumlin and Crindau.

Today the canal ends at Cwmcarn, for a new road to Crumlin was constructed along the route of the canal in the 1970s. During the canal era, Cwmcarn was the point where loads were transferred to the canal from the Aberbeerg and Beaufort tramways which followed the two arms of the Ebbw to the ironworks at the heads of the valleys.

A reservoir was constructed at Cwmcarn to supply water to the Crumlin arm of the Monmouthshire Canal. It was built soon after the canal was started and was known as Roger's Pond.

On Wednesday 14 July 1875, very heavy rain caused the reservoir to burst its banks, sending thousands of tons of water cascading down into the Carne Valley. The rush of water gathered such momentum that when it reached the turnpike road it 'ponded back' in a hollow and then enveloped a cottage where the Davis family lived. Father, daughter and son were drowned, while the cottage was submerged, with the water rising in the hollow to a depth of forty feet. It then gushed forward making a breach in the canal embankment forty yards wide.

The force of the water then continued to destroy a substantially built house which adjoined the local flannel factory. Eight members of the Hunt family who lived there were drowned, with the exception of Mr. Hunt who was washed into the branches of a tree. It was some hours before he was rescued but he was so shocked and badly injured that he died soon afterwards.

An inquest into the cause of the tragedy revealed that for many years before the accident, the reservoir had been neglected and allowed to fall into disrepair.

The canal terminated near the Navigation Inn at Crumlin and was slightly shortened when the Crumlin Viaduct was built with one pier standing in the actual canal. Today there is no sign of the canal, but the Navigation Inn has survived.

Pen y Fan Pond which is situated in the hills high above Crumlin was built to provide water for the canal. It is now the centrepiece of a popular Country Park.

EASTERN ARM

The eastern arm of the Monmouthshire Canal runs for 11 miles between Newport and Pontnewynydd rising 447 feet through 42 locks. Near the 5 Locks at Pontrhydyrhun a tunnel was constructed 260 feet in length, which the bargees had to 'walk' their boats through by pushing with their feet on the tunnel walls. This arm of the canal was opened in 1796 and within three years the two branches of the Monmouthshire Canal were carrying a total of 29,000 tons of coal and 12,000 tons of iron. The 64 ft. barge with its 25 ton load would take a whole day to travel the 11 miles from Pontnewynydd to Newport. Undoubtedly the Monmouthshire Canal was handicapped by the number of locks necessary on both arms of the canal. The section of canal from Pontymoile to Pontnewynydd with its 11 locks was always short of water. Its abandonment was authorised under Acts of 1843 and 1848 but it was not closed until 1849. In 1854 it was filled in and converted to a railway.

In 1854 the Monmouthshire Canal was cut short in Newport by half-a-mile with the result that it terminated at Canal Parade instead of Potter Street. Nine years later it was shortened again to finish at Llanarth Street.

From 1860 the canal rapidly went into decline. The very same people who had bought shares in the Canal Company now looked to the railways for the next stage of expansion and formed the Monmouthshire Railway and Canal Company. Coal was the primary resource in demand and it could be more efficiently transported to Newport by rail.

In 1930 a further section of the canal in Newport was closed when the waterway was terminated at High Street Bridge although a culvert still carried water from this point to the Town Dock until it too closed.

Gwastad Lock, near Malpas has been restored to working order by Newport Borough Council. It has had new gates fitted but it is necessary to pump the water to the upper pound when the lock operation is being demonstrated to educational parties. There is a car park nearby.

THE GROWTH OF NEWPORT

With the coming of the canal, and the associated tramroads which brought iron, limestone and timber from the upper parts of the valleys to the barges, the industrial life of the area, particularly Newport, was

Opposite: *A well known view of Pensarn bridge looking up part of the flight of 14 locks ascending Cefn Hill at Rogerstone. On the right can be seen the lock-keeper's cottage which was occupied in quite recent years by Jack Brooks who claimed to have brought the last narrow boat down from Crumlin in 1930.*

transformed. Iron was needed for making cannon to use against Napoleon, while Coal was increasingly required for use in ships, steam engines and domestic heating. Between 1800 and 1810 the population of Newport doubled and 150,000 tons of coal a year were being exported. When the chain of ironworks sprang up along the heads of the valleys and the value of the coal that lay hidden in the hills in the west of Monmouthshire was realised, the growth of Newport was very rapid. Due to its situation near the mouth of the tidal Usk and also its close proximity to the coalfield, Newport was to become one of the great trading ports of South Wales.

In the early days, coal and iron were brought to the wharves of Newport by the Monmouthshire Canal, but as trade increased and the tramroads prepared the way for the railways, better provision for loading ships was required than that offered by the riverside wharves. In 1842 the Town Dock was opened but a continued increase in trade and the introduction of larger vessels, led to further dock extension.

In 1875 the Alexandra Dock was opened, to which the South Dock was added in 1893. Further extensions included a new entrance, to this the largest dock in the world, capable of accomodating the biggest ships afloat.

A series of panels set into the walls of the Old Green interchange near Newport Castle provide an interesting and colourful portrayal of the history of the canal and tramroad system which gave rise to the development of Newport.

Brief history of the Monmouthire Canal

1792	Act of Parliament gives permission to cut the Monmouthshire Canal.
1796	The Newport - Pontnewynydd section is opened.
1798	The Newport to Crumlin section is opened.
1812	Brecknock & Abergavenny and the Monmouthshire Canals are joined at Pontymoile.
1830	600,000 tons of coal, iron etc are carried on the Monmouthshire Canal.
1845	816,905 tons of coal, iron etc are carried on the Monmouthshire Canal.
1852	Newport to Pontypool Railway is opened.
1854	Newport Docks Company obtains powers to take water from the Monmouthshire Canal at Newport.
1868	57,000 tons of coal, iron etc are carried on the Monmouthshire Canal.
1879	Canal is closed below Llanarth Street in Newport.
1880	Great Western Railway takes over the Monmouthshire Railway & Canal Company.
1930	Last cargo boat travels from Crumlin to Newport. A section of the canal in Newport is destroyed by the Kingsway road scheme.
1938	Last cargo boat travels from Newport to Pontymoile.
1949	Crumlin arm of the canal closes.
1954	A British Transport Commission Act authorises the closure of 3 miles of the Monmouthshire Canal at Cwmbran New Town.
1962	Eastern arm of the canal is abandoned.
1976	14 Locks Canal Centre/Picnic Site opens to the public.

Opposite: Junction Cottage at Pontymoile Basin was built by William Jones, a local tradesman for the Brecknock & Abergavenny Canal Company in 1814. It was occupied by a man whose job it was to look after the locks, keep the waterways clear and gauge the weight of the barges. It was designed so that there were three directions of vision on the canal. From the basin a canal branch originally went up to Pontypool and Pontnewynydd but this was closed and it became the route of the MR & CCo's railway from Newport to Pontypool from 1852.

THE BRECKNOCK AND ABERGAVENNY CANAL

Notice was first given of the proposal to construct an 'Abergavenny' canal at a meeting held in August 1792. Originally it was planned to build the lower section of this canal from the River Usk at Caerleon, to follow the river valley past Llangibby and Abergavenny to reach Gilwern and the Llangrwyney ironworks.

The following month at a second meeting it was decided to extend the route of the proposed canal to Brecon and it accordingly became known as the 'Brecknock & Abergavenny Canal'. However, before long, the Monmouthshire Canal Company stepped in and offered £3,000 to the B & A Co. to abandon this route and join their canal at Pontymoile instead. As a result of this change of plan the Engineer, Thomas Dadford Jnr. surveyed a route of 33 miles from Pontymoile to Brecon and also routes for three connecting tramroads. He surveyed from Gilwern up the valley of the Clydach to Beaufort, from Abergavenny wharf (Llanfoist) to Abergavenny bridge and from Gilwern to Glangrwyney.

The first meeting of the shareholders took place at the 'Golden Lion' in Brecon on the 16, March 1793. A few share-holders of the Monmouthshire Company, were also present, including Sir Charles Morgan, the Duke of Beaufort, the Hanburys of Pontypool and the Homfray brothers. An Act passed in 1793 gave power to build tramroads up to eight miles from the canal. It provided capital of £100,000, with the sum of £50,000 in reserve.

In 1797 construction of the canal began with the building of an aqueduct which would carry the waterway over the River Clydach as part of the first section heading from Gilwern towards Brecon.

92

By March 1799 the canal was completed from Gilwern to Talybont on Usk and progressing well towards Brecon. The canal reached Brecon in 1800. Two further sections were then started. The first from Gilwern to Llanfoist, was completed in 1805 by Thomas Cartwright and the final link joining the B & A to the Monmouthshire Canal was built from Llanfoist to Pontymoile by William Crosley. He had previously been engineer to the Rochdale Canal and was appointed by the B & A Company in 1809, at a salary of £500 a year. His instructions were to complete the work within three years. He managed to achieve this target, with assistance from John Hodgkinson who surveyed the route down to Pontymoile. In today's terms it was almost the equivalent of building the Channel Tunnel. The final connection was made with the Monmouthshire Canal at Bridge 52, just below Junction Cottage.

Savings had been made by building the canal along a route which followed the natural contours, thus avoiding the need for numerous locks. Only six locks and one tunnel were in fact needed on its entire length. The main engineering problems were at Gilwern where the canal crossed the River Clydach and at Brynich, where an aqueduct had to be built over the River Usk.

In 1845, 816,905 tons of coal and iron were transported along the B & A and the Monmouthshire Canals to Newport Docks. Timber and agricultural produce was also carried. Limestone for use as an agricultural fertiliser was taken in the other direction to Brecon. The B & A and the Monmouthshire Canals were taken over by the Great Western Railway in 1880.

Opposite: *This picture shows the construction of the Gilwern Aqueduct in 1797 by the Canal Engineer Thomas Dadford Jnr. It was necessary to build this massive embankment and aqueduct to bridge the Clydach Gorge.*

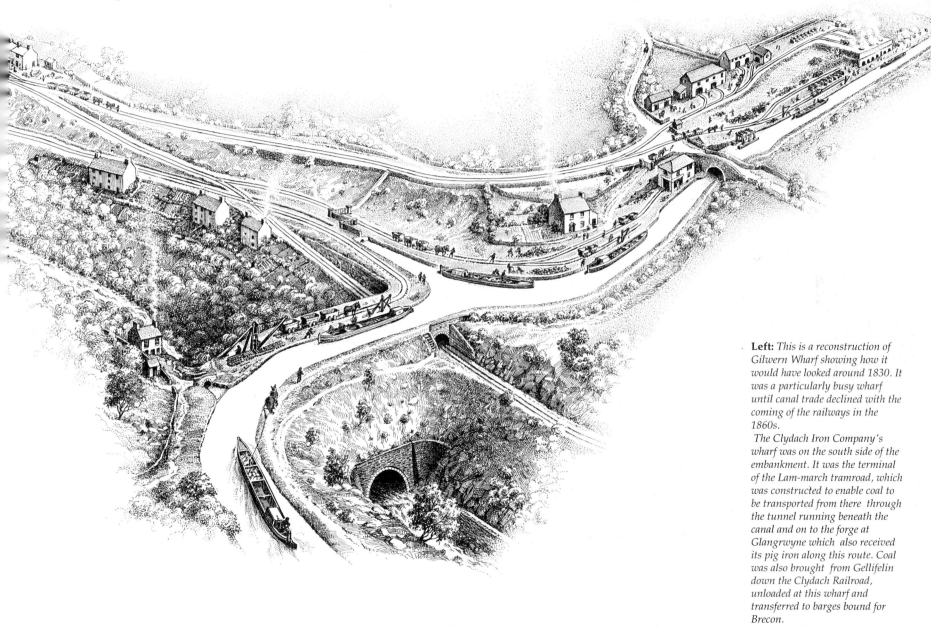

Left: *This is a reconstruction of Gilwern Wharf showing how it would have looked around 1830. It was a particularly busy wharf until canal trade declined with the coming of the railways in the 1860s.*

The Clydach Iron Company's wharf was on the south side of the embankment. It was the terminal of the Lam-march tramroad, which was constructed to enable coal to be transported from there through the tunnel running beneath the canal and on to the forge at Glangrwyne which also received its pig iron along this route. Coal was also brought from Gellifelin down the Clydach Railroad, unloaded at this wharf and transferred to barges bound for Brecon.

Right: *Loading timber at Gilwern Wharf.*

Opposite: *An aqueduct at Govilon on the Brecknock & Abergavenny Canal.*

A brief history of the Brecknock & Abergavenny Canal

1792   Notice is given of a proposal for an 'Abergavenny Canal' at a meeting in August to run from the Llangrwyney Ironworks to just below Usk. A further meeting in September decides to extend the canal to Brecon and it thus becomes known as the 'Brecknock & Abergavenny Canal'.
In October the Monmouthshire Canal Company offers the Brecknock & Abergavenny Company £3,000 if they join their Newport to Pontnewynydd branch at Pontymoile instead of the River Usk.

1793   Act of Parliament authorising the construction of the B & A Canal. The first shareholders' meeting is held on 16 May in the Golden Lion, Brecon.

1794   The Clydach Railroad from Gelli felin Colliery to Gilwern and on by a bridge over the River Usk to Glangrwyney Ironworks is built by the Brecknock & Abergavenny Company.
(The bridge was destroyed by a flood in 1795.)
The Monmouthshire Company pays £3,000 to the B & A Company in March and pushes for the canal to be started.

1796   Thomas Dadford Jnr. is appointed as Engineer on a part-time basis.

1797   Canal construction is started at Gilwern when a contract is let for the building of an aqueduct and embankment.

1797   By November the 8 miles stretch from Gilwern to Llangynidr is completed.

1798   Thomas Dadford is made full-time Engineer.

1799   By February it is completed to Talybont.

1800   On Dec 24 the last stretch to Brecon is opened.

1802   In March it is decided to extend the canal down to Llanfoist - the proposed site of the Abergavenny Wharf.

1804   An Act allows the Company to raise an additional £80,000 - either by loan or by the creation of new shares. Eventually the Company has to borrow an additional £50,000 from other sources.

1805   The canal reaches Llanfoist.

1812   On 8 February the entire length of the B & A Canal is opened to traffic and the link between Newport and Brecon is complete.

1845   The Newport to Pontypool Railway Act is passed.

1849   Consideration is given to laying a railway track along the towpath of the B & A Canal from Brecon to Pontypool, but following a survey no action is taken.

1851   A proposed Breconshire Railway to Abergavenny offers to buy the canal. The B & A Company states a price of £105,750, but the proposal is dropped.

1860   Part of the canal above Llanfoist collapses and a section of the lower incline is washed away. The incline is no longer used after this date.

1864   An Act is passed authorising the construction of a railway from Abergavenny to Crickhowell.
The B & A Company is purchased by the Monmouthshire Railway & Canal Company

1880   On 1 August the Monmouthshire Railway & Canal Company amalgamates with the Great Western Railway who use the canal for short hauls until 1930.

1933   The last toll is taken on the B & A Canal at Llangynidr.

1948   Nationalisation of the railways means that the GWR no longer administer the offices of the canal. The British Transport Commission is formed and it takes over the responsibility for canals.

1963   Management of canals passes to the British Waterways Board.
Govilon Boat Club - the first inland cruising club in Wales is formed and pleasure use of the canal starts in earnest.

1968   Breconshire and Monmouthshire County Councils make an agreement with the British Waterways Board under the National Parks and Access to the Countryside Act 1949 to meet one-half of the cost of restoration and subsequent maintenance of the Monmouthshire & Brecon Canal.

1970   On 16 October the B & A Canal is officially re-opened for navigation from Pontymoile to Brecon (32 miles) by the Minister of State for Wales.

1975   Major breach occures in the embankment at Llanfoist.

1981   Repairs are completed and the canal is re-opened.

1994   Breach occurs at Talybont-on-Usk.

1995   Navigation is restored to Crown Bridge Pontypool.

Opposite: This illustration shows the Llanfihangel Tramroad and the Brecknock & Abergavenny Canal at Govilon. It also shows a spur off the tramroad which terminated a few hundred yards further on. This reconstruction was created from evidence of a few yards of trackwork being unearthed completely in situ in a garden next to the canal. The Llanfihangel Tramroad ran from Govilon to Hereford.

RAILROADS AND TRAMROADS

Transport to the ironworks and from them to the coast was originally by packhorse, but this was obviously far too slow and costly for the rapidly expanding iron industry.

One mule could carry three hundredweight (151 kilos) in panniers without difficulty. Its working life was 25 years compared to 20 for a horse. Pack horses and mules operated in teams of twelve and the total load was known as 'a dozen'.

When the Monmouthshire Canal was completed in 1798 the situation was eased for a while, particularly once it was linked by horse-drawn tramways to the various ironworks, collieries and quarries.

These tramroads provided vital links between the ironworks and the canals and also enabled ironstone, coal and limestone to be transported from their extraction sites to the ironworks. In subsequent years they also provided connections with the collieries.

Tramroads used L shaped plates, known as plateways which were laid to guide the wheels, whilst a railroad had bar rails which were designed to take flanged wheels.

Archdeacon Coxe came to Blaenafon in 1798 and witnessed the construction of a railroad:

In the vicinity of Blaenavon we observed the process of making a railroad, so called because it is formed by a kind of frame with iron rails, or bars, laid lengthways, and fastened or cramped by means of cross-bars. The ground being excavated, about 6ft. in breadth, and by 2 ft. in depth, is strewed over with broken pieces of stone and the frame laid down; it is composed of rails, sleepers, or cross-bars, and under-sleepers. The rail is a bar of cast iron, 4 ft. in length, 2 in. thick and 1 in broad, its extremities are repectively concave and convex, or, in other words, are morticed and tenoned into each other, and fastened at the ends by two wooden pegs to a cross-bar called the sleeper. The sleeper was originally of iron, but experience having shown that iron was liable to snap or bend, it is now made of wood, which is considerably cheaper, and requires less repair. Under each extremity of the sleeper is a square piece of wood, called the under-sleeper, to which it is attached by a peg. The frame being thus laid down and filled with stones, gravel and earth, the iron rails form a ridge over the surface, over which the wheels of the car glide by means of iron grooved rims, 3.in. broad. This is the general structure of the road when carried in a straight line; at the junction of two roads, and to facilitate the passage of two cars in opposite directions, moveable rails, called turn rails are occasionally used, which are fastened with screws instead of pegs, and may be pushed sideways. The level of the ground is taken with great exactness, and the declevity in general so gentle as to be almost imperceptible... The expense of forming these roads is very considerable, varying according to the nature of the ground, and the difficulty or facility of procuring proper materials; it is seldom less than a thousand pounds per mile, and sometimes exceeds that sum.'

The use of stone blocks as sleepers was recommended in 1799 by Benjamin Outram who described the technique as follows:

'The ground is first formed in the best manner the nature of it will admit, and perfectly drained; then covered with a bed of small stone or good gravel, six inches in thickness, and four

Left: *Example of a plateway. used on the early tram roads. The L-shaped lengths of iron were designed to guide smooth and non flanged wheels They were laid on blocks of stone and fastened in place with iron spikes driven into oak plugs inserted in the block holes.*

yards in breadth, for a single road, and six yards for a double one; on this bed, stamped firm, are placed blocks of stone for sleepers for the rails; each block being upwards of one cwt.; in the centre of each block a circular hole is drilled six inches deep, and in it is put an octagonal plug of oak five inches long, which receives an iron spike, that fastens down the ends of the two rails that rest upon the block, the spaces between the blocks are filled with small stones, which are rammed close about the blocks, and covered with gravel, but not so high as the soles of the rails outside, nor so high as the top of the flanches on the inside between the rails...'

The word tram probably comes from the name of the engineer Outram who was responsible for many of the tramroads in this area. In 1799 he was asked to survey the Monmouthshire Canal Company's lines, and in his report he commented:-

'The railways to Beaufort and Blaenafon are better laid out than most I have seen on that system. The Trosnant road should have been constructed on a more gradual gradient, but they are all constructed on a principle far inferior to the system I have and which after several years proof in a great variety of situations has been found to exceed every other make hitherto adopted. The labour of one horse on a railway of this kind being equal to the labour of four horses on the best railways that have been constructed on the plan of those belonging to the Monmouthshire Canal Company.'

The 'rules of the road' laid down by the Canal Company were few and simple. No waggon must have less than four wheels; their speed was not to exceed four miles an hour; empty waggons always had to give way to loaded waggons, and, after mid-day, loaded waggons going down had to make way for loaded waggons going up.

Two types of rail were described in 1825 by the engineer George Overton who built the famous Pen y Darren Tramroad:

'On the edge-railway the rims of the carriage are made broad, with a flanch on the side of the wheels to prevent the carriage from leaving the rails, which renders the carriage or waggon considerably heavier than the tram...(alternatively) the wheels of the tram are narrow in the rim, coming nearly to an edge; and there is a flanch on the inner side of the plate upon which they move to prevent the carriages or trams from running off the road.'

Not everyone was in favour of the construction of tramroads. In particular the Rev Augustus Morgan who wrote in 1847:-

In my opinion a tramroad for the conveyance of coal from the hills tends to demoralise the district through which it passes to an inconceivable degree. The results are theft, drunkeness and prostitution. Women and children of all ages, sent out by their parents, are seen at all hours following trams to obtain by any means except pecuniary purchase, coals for the use of their respective families.'

After the application of Cort's patents and other improvements the cost of producing rails fell and this led to an increase in the building of railroads. These roads were about 4 feet wide, the heavy rails being pegged down to long wooden sleepers and on to large flat stones with holes drilled in them. Upon this pair of rails ran bulky trolleys or waggons with box-like wooden bodies fitted upon flanged iron rails. They carried loads ranging from 1 - 6 tons and were pulled by mules, but on steep inclines the self-acting principle of a controlled descent by gravity was adopted. Their speed and the quantity of the material they carried easily exceeded that of the canal barge.

Many blacksmiths and farriers did little else but shoe horses or repair the iron parts of waggons, and in the nineteenth century the horse was so highly valued that the penalty for stealing one was death by hanging. There is a record of a horse thief being followed from Llanellen to Talgarth where he was caught and later hanged at Usk prison. He was the last man to die there for that offence.

Right: *Example of an edge-rail used as a lintel over a culvert on the Clydach Railroad.*

Samuel Homfray was so proud of his teams of tramroad horses that he commissioned a portrait of his favourite team and it was prominently displayed in Bedwellty House, Tredegar. This painting is now in the National Museum of Wales and it bears the legend:

'A plain representation of the Team and Trams of coal brought down to Pillgwenlly by Samuel Homfray Esq., on Tuesday, 18 December 1821. Weight of coal, 79 tons, 10 cwt.

To Samuel Homfray Esq. The Independent Iron Master and Coal Merchant whose exertions have benefitted the town and neighbourhood of Newport by reducing the price of coal. This piece is Humbly Inscribed by his Humble Servant John Thomas.'

Two teams of four white horses are shown hauling trams filled with coal. Samuel Homfray can be seen sitting on a chair on the first tram holding a silver cup on his knees. In the background is the sea with several sailing ships.

In 1791 not a single yard of railroad existed in South Wales, but between 1800 and 1830 several hundred miles were constructed. It would have been possible to take the longest tramroad journey in the world if one travelled from the head of the Monmouthshire Canal at Crumlin to Nantyglo, then on to Brynmawr, down Bailey's Tramroad to Govilon and then on, by the Llanfihangel Tramroad to Hereford - a total distance of nearly 100 miles.

Monmouthshire Tramroads and Railroads

Aberbeeg Tramroad

This tramroad was constructed in 1828 and ran for a distance of just under 6 miles on the eastern side of the Ebbw Fach river from Aberbeeg to the Coalbrookvale Works of George Brewer & Co. A private tramroad then continued to Nantyglo to connect with Bailey's Tramroad.

Bailey's Tramroad

In 1804 the construction of a tramroad from Nantyglo Ironworks, through the Clydach Gorge and down to Govilon Wharf was authorised. Work started in 1819 and the 5 mile tramroad which became known as Bailey's Tramroad (named after Crawshay Bailey), was completed in 1821. In later years it became the route of the Abergavenny to Brynmawr railway.

Beaufort Tramroad

This was just under 6 miles long and ran from Gilwern to Beaufort and was built in 1796.

Blaenafon Tramroad

Constructed in 1795 by Thomas Dadford Jnr., the Blaenafon Tramroad ran for 5 miles from the Blaenafon Ironworks to the canal head at Pontnewynydd. There were branches on its western side to ironworks and collieries at Cwmffrwd, Varteg and Abersychan.

It was built of iron rails bolted to large stones weighing 3 to 4 cwts which were used as sleepers. The driver, when descending the track, would hitch his horse to the rear of the waggon in places where the gradient allowed, enabling the tram to run under its own steam. On the return journey the horse pulled the empty trams.

When the Monmouthshire Canal was linked with the Breconshire waterway, use of the Blaenafon tramroad declined, for loads were then sent via Hill's Tramroad to Llanfoist Wharf. The reason being that the Canal Company were now compelled to accept traffic at Pontymoel Junction at the same rates previously charged by the Brecon Canal and it thus became more economic to go this way.

Left: *Typical tramroad scene*

Blaendare Tramroad ————————

Built by Thomas Dadford Jnr. in 1796 this 1 mile tramroad ran from Pontymoile to Blaendare Ironworks. It was later extended to Blaen y Cwm.

Bryn Oer Tramroad ————————

Initiated by Benjamin Hall this tramroad was constructed in 1815 from Buckland House Wharf at Talybont-on-Usk up the Caerfanell valley to the head of the Dyffryn Crawnon and then on to Bryn Oer near Rhymney. It was later extended to Trefil Quarries and on to Benjamin Hall's Rhymney Ironworks, a total distance of 12 miles.

Clydach Railroad ————————

In 1793 an Act was passed authorising the construction of '...*a Rail or Waggon Way or Stone Road to be built from Wain Dew, between Brynmawr and Beaufort, past the Llanelly Furnace to the canal at Aberclydach (Gilwern).*' It was built in 1794 by John Dadford, brother of Thomas Dadford and it became known as the Clydach Railroad. The rails were purchased from the Penydarren Ironworks, Merthyr Tydfil.

'A short but steep railroad of 4 miles, with a gradient of 1 in 12 at the Black Rock, took the loaded trams down the Clydach Valley from the mouth of the levels to the wharves at Llanelly, and then a fleet of 16 Canal Boats of 21 tons burden each, conveyed the coal to Brecon, a distance of 18 miles, and the Company were able to sell there at 14s. a ton, though the profit was small. All the countryside came for their supply of coal, and in the late Autumn every farmer came and fetched his stock of coal from the Brecon Boat Company's Wharf. And further afield, to Herefordshire and Radnorshire, coal was delivered from this Wharf to traders like Benjamin Trusted the Quaker of Hay, and William Bridgwater of Glasbury, along the Hay and Eardisley Tramroad. In severe frosts there was great interruption to the Canal traffic, but the yard at Brecon was always well stocked for winter against the chance of severe frosts occuring.'

J. Lloyd, *Early History of the Old South Wales Iron Works, 1760-1840*

The Clydach Railroad passed through a tunnel running beneath the canal at Gilwern Wharf and continued from there to Glangrwyne Forge which received its pig iron along this route. (From the Corn Exchange, Gilwern to Glangrwyney it is now a road. It was made into a parish road in 1833, two years after the closure of Glangrwyne Forge). Coal was also brought from Gellifelin, unloaded at Brynmawr and transferred to barges bound for Brecon.

It was extended in 1794 to Brynmawr, with a branch to the colliery at Llwydcoed and another to Nantyglo Ironworks. The following year it was extended from Brynmawr to Beaufort and then on to Rhyd-y-Blew, where it joined the Trefil Tramroad.

Craig yr Hafod Tramroad ————————

Constructed in 1799 this tramroad was 4 miles long and ran from Graig yr Hafod Quarry on Mynydd Garn Fawr (south east of the Blorenge) down to Twyn Glais Bridge where a lime kiln was constructed beside the B & A Canal. The route involved a total descent of about 900 feet.

Ebbw Vale Tramroad ————————

Constructed in 1796 by G. Boye this 8 mile tramroad ran from Crumlin Bridge to Beaufort Ironworks.

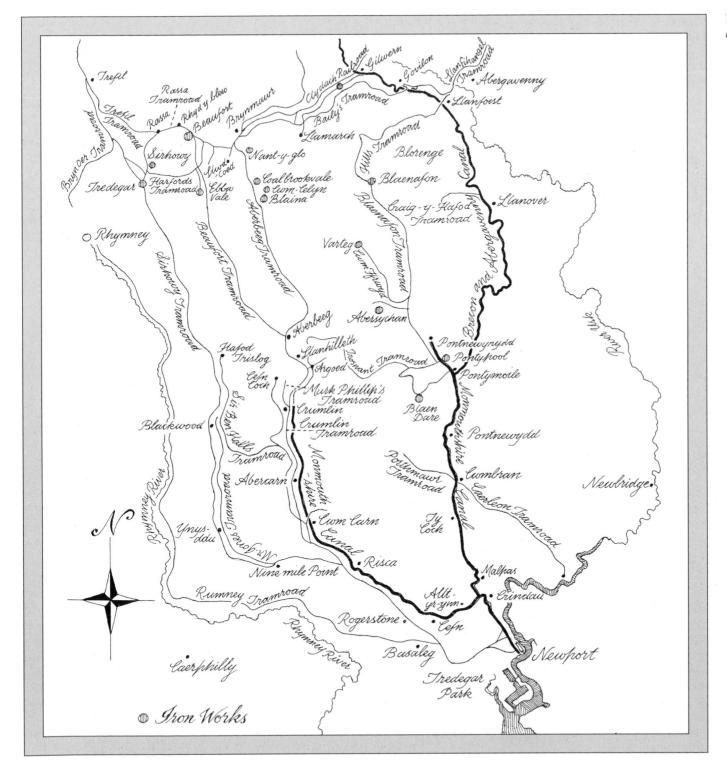

Trefil

Rassa Tramroad
Rassa
Rhyd y bleu
Beaufort
Brynmawr

Clydach Railroad
Gilwern
Govilon
Llanvihangel Tramroad
Abergavenny
Llanfoist

Trefil Tramroad
Baily's Tramroad

Bryn Oer Tramroad
Sirhowy
Llanarch
Hills Tramroad
Blorenge

Tredegar
Harfords Tramroad
Llwyd Coed
Ebbw Vale
Nant-y-glo
Coalbrookvale
Cwm-celyn
Blaina

Blaenafon
Craig-y-Hafod Tramroad
Llanover

Rhymney

Sirhowy Tramroad
Beaufort Tramroad
Ebbw Vale
Varteg
Cwm Ffrwyd

Blaenafon Tramroad

Brecon and Abergavenny Canal

Aberbeeg
Abersychan

Hafod Trislog
Llanhilleth
Argoed
Trosnant Tramroad
Pontnewynydd
Pontypool
Pontymoile

Cefn Coch
Murk Phillip's Tramroad
Crumlin
Crumlin Tramroad
Blaen Dare

Blackwood
Sir Ben Hall's Tramroad

Pontnewydd
Pontymawr Tramroad
Cwmbran
Newbridge

Abercarn
Monmouthshire
Ty Coch
Monmouthshire Canal
Caerleon Tramroad

Ynys-ddu
Mr Jones Tramroad
Cwm Carn
Canal
Risca

Nine mile Point

Rumney Tramroad
Rogerstone
Cefn
Malpas
Allt-yr-ynn
Crindau

Rhymney River
Basaleg
Newport

Caerphilly
Tredegar Park

River Usk

N

⬤ Iron Works

Cwmffrwd Railroad

This was the only gravity operated incline established by the Monmouthshire Canal Company in the Eastern Valley. The trams, each weighing about 17 cwts and carrying three tons, were drawn in trains of 20 to 24 by horses. Braking was applied by inserting 'sprags' in the skeleton of the wheel. The steep gradient of this railroad made it unsuitable for use by locomotive engines in later years.

Grosmont Tramroad

Constructed by William Crosley in 1818 this was built as a continuation of the Llanfihangel Tramroad from Llanfihangel Crucorney to Llangua Bridge - a distance of 7 miles.

Hall's Tramroad

This tramroad was built by Benjamin Hall to transport coal from his pits at Abercarn via Newbridge to the canal. It was later converted into a railway and in due course became part of the Western Region system.

Harford's Tramroad

This was built in 1818 to link the Sirhowy furnaces with the rolling mills at Ebbw Vale. It involved the construction of a tunnel through the mountain to connect the two adjacent valleys.

Hill's Tramroad

Named after Thomas Hill the ironmaster, this tramroad was built in the 1820s. It ran from Blaenafon to Pwll-du and on to the limestone quarries at Tyla. It was later extended to Llanfoist when the Garnddyrys works were built. From there it contoured around the side of the Blorenge via a tunnel and then down three inclines to reach Llanfoist Wharf on the B & A Canal. A fourth incline led down to the Llanfihangel Tramroad.

Llanfihangel Tramroad

In 1792 Thomas Dadford Jnr. put forward a plan and estimate for constructing a canal from Llanfoist via an aqueduct over the River Usk providing a waterway link with Hereford. He also proposed tramroad connections with Longtown and Turnastone. However, his ambitious plans were rejected at a meeting held at Grosmont in 1793.

Four years later a proposal was made that a tramroad should be built to link the B & A Canal with Hereford and the following year, on 26 September this scheme was formally agreed. William Crosley was then appointed to survey a possible route.

Constructed under a special Act of Parliament passed in May 1811 the Llanfihangel Tramroad was built by William Crosley at a cost of £13,390 for a single track for horse-drawn trams. It started at the wharf of the B & A Canal at Govilon. After crossing the River Usk on a stone viaduct adjacent to the old highway bridge on its west side, it curved around the north side of Abergavenny and passed near the New Inn, Mardy to terminate in a field to the east of Llanfihangel Crucorney. The total length was 7 miles and it consisted of cast iron plates 3 ft. long 4 in. wide on the tread with a vertical flange 3 in. in depth laid on stone blocks, each weighing about 120 lbs. Spikes 4 in. long were driven through a hole in the stone.

Originally it had been intended to build a tramroad from Abergavenny to Hereford to transport coal and lime to that town, but various concerns with vested interests such as barge owners obstructed this proposal. There were also schemes being put forward to make the Wye navigable as far as Hereford.

In 1812 a special Act was passed for the Grosmont tramroad which commenced at the terminal of the Llanfihangel tramroad and continued for 6 miles to Monmouth Cap at a cost of about £12,000. It was not until 1826 that a special Act was passed for the construction of the last length of the horse-drawn tramroad, between Monmouth Cap and Hereford. This final stretch was opened on 21 Sept 1829 and the first consignment of coal was delivered to Hereford from Abergavenny.

In 1843 the Newport, Abergavenny and Hereford Railway Company was formed under a special Act of Parliament to construct a steam railway between Pontypool and Hereford. At this time there were three tramroad companies operating between Abergavenny and Hereford namely: The Llanfihangel Company, The Grosmont Company and the Hereford Company. These were purchased for £21,750, £16,250 and £19,460 respectively. The three tramroads appear to have been operated by the Railway Company until the new railway to Hereford was opened on January 2, 1854.

The new railway was laid alongside the old tramroad although there were some diversions in parts, of several hundred yards.

On July 1, 1860 the Newport, Abergavenny and Hereford Railway was taken over by the West Midland Railway Company, which was soon after taken over by the Great Western Railway Company.

Llangattock Tramroad

Constructed in 1816 this tramroad connected the Nantyglo Ironworks with the Llangattock Quarries. It closed in 1911 and is now a road contouring around the hillside, providing magnificent views.

Llanhilleth Tramroad

This 2 mile tramroad was built in 1799 and ran from Crumlin Bridge via Llanhilleth Collieries to Cwm Cyffin.

Llammarch Tramroad

Built by Thomas Dadford Jnr. in 1795 this tramroad ran from Llammarch Colliery to Clydach Ironworks, a distance of nearly 2 miles. It was extended to Gilwern in 1803 by H. Hendhall.

Mamhilad to Usk Tramroad (Proposed)

An Act was passed on 16 June 1814 for a tramroad from the canal at Croes y Pant, near, Mamhilad, to Usk Bridge - just over 5 miles. The subscribers included Thomas Hill and Samuel Hopkins of Blaenafon and Watkin George of Pontypool. The engineer was to be John Hodgkinson, but the Act was not implimented.

Penllwyn Tramroad

Just over 5 miles long this tramroad of 1824, built by John Hodgkinson, ran from Blackwood to Nine Mile Point where it joined the Monmouthshire Canal Company's tramroad. The section from Nine Mile Point to Ynysddu was taken over by the Sirhowy Tramroad Company and renamed Llanarth Tramroad. Some interesting features still to be seen are the Pont Gam ('Crooked Bridge') which spans the Afon Sirhowy at Gelligroes and the old weighing office and counting house which is now the 'Rock and Fountain' Inn at Penmaen.

Ponthir and Caerleon Tramroad

The quay at Caerleon used to be the terminus of the Ponthir and Caerleon tramroad which was built to carry iron ore and tinplate from the Caerleon and Ponthir Tinplate Works to the wharf for shipment to Bristol. Originally the tramroad was built to connect Caerleon Forge with the wharf, but it was extended to link with the Monmouthshire Canal at Halfway House, Cwmbran. By about 1865 the tramroad went out of use.

Porthmawr Tramroad

Built in 1799, this 2 mile tramroad ran from Halfway House, Cwmbran to Mynydd Maen Collieries.

Rassau Tramroad

Constructed in 1797 to connect Sirhowy Ironworks with Beaufort Ironworks 3 miles away, the Rassau Tramroad was probably the first and thus the oldest long distance tramroad in the world. It was financed by Richard Fothergill and built by Thomas Dadford Jnr.

The Rassau Tramroad formed the middle section of line to Trefil Quarries providing a link to Sirhowy brickworks. But its main purpose was to cross the hillside to the new Beaufort Furnace where it linked with another tramroad which ran through the Ebbw Valley and down to the canal head at Crumlin.

The Rhyd-y-Blew inn was a coaching house in the 18th century and it stands on the route of the Rassau Tramroad. Horses kept in the stables for the stage coaches were also made available for use on the tramroad.

Rumney Tramroad

Engineered by Geoge Overton this tramroad was built in 1826 with a gauge of 4 feet 2 inches and it ran for nearly 22 miles from the Rhymney Ironworks down the east bank of the River Rhymney to near Machen. From there it continued in an easterly direction to link with the Monmouthshire Tramroad from Newport at the top end of the Park Mile. The route involved a height difference of 756 ft. Between 1840 and 1845 locomotive engines were introduced and in 1863 the line was vested in the Brecon & Merthyr Railway Company.

Sirhowy Tramroad

The Sirhowy Tramroad was partly constructed in accordance with the powers granted to the promoters of the Monmouthshire Canal and it can be considered to be one of the most important of the South Wales tramroads. The 16 mile Nine Mile Point section to Sirhowy Ironworks section was built in 1805 by John Hodgkinson. The connection with Newport was completed in 1811 and the full route then connected Newport with Tredegar Ironworks and was about 28 miles in length.

A long stone viaduct was built at Risca to carry the tramroad across the Ebbw Valley to the level of the canal. It was an impressive construction, 40 - 50 feet high with thirty five arches and it is remembered by the 'Bridge End Inn' which as the name suggests stood at one end of the viaduct. Unfortunately the viaduct became unsafe and was demolished at the end of the nineteenth century. A row of houses, near the River Ebbw, nostalgically named Bridge Street was built from the stones.

In 1817 hauliers John Davies and David Williams drove the first horse-drawn train transporting coal for export down to Newport and the event was described by one reporter as follows:

'Twelve carriages were loaded and brought to the surface, some of the lumps of coal weighed several tons. On the day appointed two teams of splendid grey horses, each team consisting of four beautiful animals fully equipped and decorated, started with six carriages for each team, the huge masses of coal were decorated with flags of various colours and arrived safely at their destination to the satisfaction of the proprietors and to the astonishment of the large and interested crowd.'

In 1822 a 'passenger service' was introduced by John Kingston who 'plied' between Newport and Tredegar, paying sixpence at each tollgate. The passengers were conveyed in a special horse-drawn vehicle known as the 'caravan'.

The section that passed through the Tredegar Park Estate was known as the Golden Mile, for Sir Charles Morgan collected a toll of 1d per ton per mile. It earned him an income of £14,000 during the period 1830-40.

Trefil Tramroad

The Trefil Tramroad was established by Jeremiah Homfray (Ebbw Vale), Fothergill and Monkhouse (Sirhowy) and Daniel Williams (Beaufort). Four miles in length, it ran from Tredegar Ironworks via Nantybwch and Mountain Air to the Trefil Quarries.

Blaen y Cwm Viaduct, known locally as the 'Nine Arches,' was built to support the old Trefil Tramroad which was initially worked by horses. The name of Trefil means 'home of the mules' and this was once the most important limestone quarry in Monmouthshire. Limestone was extracted here for use as a flux in the iron smelting process. The Tredegar Company built Shop Row and the Rhymney Company erected Rhymney Terrace to house the workers employed in the quarrying of limestone. This quarry not only supplied the Tredegar and Sirhowy Ironworks but also works at Beaufort, Rhymney and Ebbw Vale.

Trefil Tramroad was later converted by the Ebbw Vale Company into a standard gauge railway which reached an altitude of 1,600 feet above sea level. In 1890 more than 35,000 tons of limestone were hauled by locomotives along this line which was in use up until 1964.

Trosnant Tramroad

Built in 1796 by Thomas Dadford Jnr. this 1 mile tramroad connected Pontypool with Old Furnace. It was extended by John Hodgkinson in 1910 to Pontymoile, making it a total length of 1.5 miles.

Tyla Quarry Tramroad

Built in 1789 this tramroad ran from Blaenafon Ironworks to Pwlldu and Tyla quarries, a distance of just over 2 miles.

Varteg Tramroad

Built in 1819 this 3 mile tramroad ran from Cwmavon to No. I Colliery on Varteg Hill and Varteg Ironworks.

COAL MINING IN MONMOUTHSHIRE

Coal extraction between the thirteenth and fifteenth centuries was mainly done by 'patching', or digging the horizontal seams in open workings where the coal outcrops at the surface. In many places the early workings were bell-pits, a shallow pit being dug near the outcrop of a seam and workings being made outwards from it in all directions, until it was considered to be unsafe to proceed, when a similar pit would be dug further along the outcrop. When a seam outcropped on a steep hillside, slants and levels were carried out for a short distance. This allowed the miner to reach the coal and also provided an outlet for the water. The excavated coal was loaded into baskets which were pushed or dragged to the surface. These levels were often driven without any idea of ventilation and, the further they went into the hillside, the more difficult they were to work. When the percentage of gas became too high, the workings were abandoned and allowed to fall in.

At the beginning of the eighteenth century, coal was sold at the mine entrance for as little as two shillings a ton, but by the end of the century the price had doubled.

When coal converted into coke started being used as a fuel in the ironworking process, it was given a new importance and demand increased. Coal was then seen as an industry in its own right and the output trebled in the decade following 1840.

Coal mining in its inception was merely an auxiliary process to the iron-making industry. The steam engine, however, was to find another purpose for this fuel and to create a demand for Welsh coal which those who first used it little suspected. The lower measures of South Wales coal consist almost entirely of carbon and only a small proportion of bitumen, which means that this coal is a kind of natural coke which does not flame when ignited. It was therefore invaluable for both smelting purposes and for steam. Generally it was referred to as 'Steam Coal' to distinguish it from the bituminous flaming coal of the Midlands and the North of England.

Commencing as little more than a subsidiary to the working of ironstone, the coal industry was to become the largest and most important business in the whole of South Wales. Western Monmouthshire was rapidly converted from a land of richly wooded valleys with clean, swift-flowing rivers, inhabited by scattered farming folk, to one of the most concentrated hives of British industry. Into these narrow valleys workers poured in their thousands from the adjacent rural areas of Wales, England and Ireland. Attracted by the prospect of work and higher wages they were all absorbed in the coal, iron and associated industries.

Two-storey houses were built in rows from twenty to fifty in number, one up and one down, often terraced on steep hillsides. Such buildings were industrial barracks with each row really being just one building with partitions between the dwellings. On the whole the mining communities who lived in these valleys were happy for they were bound together by a spirit of comradeship, that was constantly nutured by shared hardship and tragedy.

Miners generally worked a 6 day, 72 hour week. On Saturdays they began work at midnight in order to finish earlier. In 1821 pay for a farm labourer was about 1 shilling per day but a miner could earn double that amount. In 1841 at Ebbw Vale they were earning 3/- per day, but by 1832 this was reduced to 2/10d. By 1839 their wages had risen again to 3/8d per day.

While men hewed the coal, women were employed to draw and push trams along levels so low that they were unable to stand upright. Children were given jobs filling trams and opening and closing underground doors to control the flow of air.

In 1841 over 45,000 men, women and children worked in the ironworks and collieries of South Wales; 10,000 of these were under 18 years of age, and 3,000 were less than 13 years old.

One of the most dangerous of jobs was that of fireman whose task was to deal with fire-damp. Covering himself with a sack cloth soaked in water he would crawl towards the gas. Lying on his stomach, he would light a candle attached to a long pole. This would be thrust into the pocket of gas and the resultant explosion would sweep over his prostrate body whilst he was

111

protected from burning by the damp sacking - in theory anyway! There was a great improvement in safety when Sir Humphrey Davy invented the safety lamp in 1815.

During his long shift the miner faced constant danger. There were haulage accidents on the roadways, falling roofs and tumbling sides caused many of the single accidents. But worst of all was the sudden catastrophe, when often a spark ignited and the whole pit was deluged in fire. A blinding flash, a roar that shook the pit and the Angel of Death took men and boys away by the hundred. Over 100,000 men, boys and women have been killed in British mines since 1850.

Prior to the development of the steam engine by Newcomen in 1712, mining could not be carried out below the level of the natural drainage; that is below the level at which underground waters would flow away, either of their own accord or by way of a narrow addit cut through to a neighbouring valley. Newcomen built his first engine at a coal mine near Dudley Castle in Staffordshire. It was a beam-engine, and a huge machine, that used low-pressure steam which meant that the boiler was little more than a giant kettle, with little risk of explosion. Because the pumps pulled water upwards it could be built at the surface instead of below ground. The invention of this machine meant that at last deep mining could be undertaken for water could now be removed. New pits were sunk and old pits that had become flooded were re-opened.

Boulton and Watt further developed Newcomen's engine, and soon steam engines were also used for hauling coal to the surface. With both these

improvements, coal levels, tunnel-like, were driven greater distances. As the uppermost layers were exhausted, the ironmasters were compelled to sink shafts to the lower measures of coal. Here, again, the steam engine was of invaluable service. Besides being used to haul materials in and out of the shafts, it was also applied to boring tools. As well as these technological advantages, knowledge of the new sciences, geology and surveying, enabled the ironmasters to obtain correct ideas of both the extent and location of the hidden coal seams.

A good circulation of air was necessary in the deep mines to prevent a build up of dangerous gases. The early method of directing a current of air through a mine was to have a fire at the bottom of one shaft to heat the air and make it rise. This started a flow of air through the workings. As collieries became deeper, more and more firedamp was found and it became dangerous to have ventilation furnaces underground. These were later replaced by large centrifrugal fans driven by steam engines located on the surface at the top of the mine shaft. This was necessary to remove firedamp, poisonous gases, caused by using explosives and carbon dioxide breathed out by men and pit ponies. The most important firm of mine ventilation fan makers in Britain was Walker Brothers of Wigan. South Wales the Waddle Patent Fan Company of Llanelli also made ventilation fans.

After 1850 the coal trade completely overshadowed the iron industry in importance. It is interesting to note that the pioneers of the coal industry, unlike the ironmasters, were themselves natives of South Wales.

Above *A typical scene in the early years of coal mining when children were employed to fill trams and open and close underground doors to control the flow of air. Child labour was made illegal by the Mines and Collieries Act of 1842.*

Left: *Sinking a new shaft was a very difficult and dangerous job and men were frequently killed.*

Coal was turned into gold, but such wealth was also accompanied by great poverty and unrest. There was still child labour at the pits, long hours with low wages, high birth and death rates, bad housing and the landscape was scarred and polluted by rubbish tips and smoke.

From 1800-1834 onwards pits were sunk in quick succession beginning in the northern outcrop coal areas at Tredegar, Blaenafon, Nantyglo, Blaina and Ebbw Vale. Development of collieries then took place in the adjoining districts of Abertilllery, Bedwellty, Pontypool, Abercarn, Risca and Cwmbran.

More than 150 collieries were scattered amongst the valleys to the west of the Usk, which gave employment to over 50,000 men in their heyday. In 1909 there were 44,298 colliers employed in Monmouthshire cutting coal and 7,175 men worked above ground attending to the engines, coke ovens etc. Numerous towns and villages owe their origin to coal mines.

Between 1846 and 1875 a series of Admiralty trials demonstrated the superiority of Welsh coal over that obtained from other mining areas in Britain, and the demand for 'smokeless Welsh' steam coal rapidly increased. This was the finest steam coal in the world, giving great heat but very little smoke, and it was particularly good for raising steam quickly in boilers. Accordingly it was not only in great demand by our own navy, but also by foreign ones as well, together with the principal shipping and railway companies, both at home and abroad.

Newport owes its importance as one of the great trading ports of South Wales to its situation near the mouth of the tidal Usk, in close proximity to the coalfield. From earliest times primitive craft had found their way into the Usk and in the days of the old sailing ships, large numbers of vessels discharged and loaded at the numerous wharves constructed along its banks.

Collieries were once scattered over the valleys above Newport in every direction from Tredegar, Ebbw Vale, Beaufort and Brynmawr in the north, to Abercarn and Risca in the south. A map drawn by John Prudeau in 1843 shows 53 collieries in Monmouthshire - 24 in the Western Valley, 21 in Sirhowy and 8 in the Eastern Valley. In later years this number increased considerably and Newport became the third largest coal-exporting port in the United Kingdom, being surpassed only by Liverpool and Cardiff.

In Monmouthshire the golden era of coal mining was from 1860-1913 and the chief centres of coal mining were at Abercarn, Abertillery, Bedwellty, Blackwood, Blaenafon, Blaina, Ebbw Vale, Nantyglo, Pontypool, Rhymney, Risca, Tredegar and Varteg.

Life Underground

One afternoon in 1995, the following conversation with two ex-miners and an electrical engineer now working as guides was recorded during their tea break at Big Pit Mining Museum, Blaenafon. All three had a family background in coal and obviously felt considerable pride in the years that they had spent working underground, just like fathers before them.

Colin Read recalled, "My father worked in the mines all his life. He is 82 now and he worked on the coal face until he was 60 years of age. My grandfather worked on the surface and also my mother's father was in the industry. So the last three generations of my family have worked in coal. I have worked in two collieries - well, three with this one"

Glyn Hallett leaned over, "Well, I have worked in five mines."

"You must have been a jinx," quipped Colin, "because they've all closed down now."

Ignoring him, Glyn continued, "My grandfather did 40 years, my father 38 years and I've done 27 and my son 15 years, I started in Beynon's at Blaina, in 1957, had a break for a while, then went into the Marine at Cwm, then moved to Merthyr Vale, then to Deep Navigation, moved again to Taff Merthyr and now I've ended up here."

Graham Gratton spoke then. "As far as I am concerned, this is my family pit. My dad was born on Good Friday in 1891. He started work at Varteg Top Pit, not far from here, just 3 days before Good Friday 1903 at the age of 12 years 11 months.

On Good Friday, 1904, he got buried under a fall - but thank goodness he was okay. He eventually retired on Good Friday in 1956.

Apart from his time at Varteg all his working life was spent here at Big Pit and for 46 years he was an official. In fact he was the Under Manager here and I will tell you how that came about. He had passed his Under-Manager paper, which was a Class 2 Examination in those days. Well, in 1913, they had a fire here, in which very sadly three officials and a dog died. The dog by the way was a rescuer's dog. But a fourth man involved in the incident was my dad. They had gone down the shaft and the manager was in the lead.

All the men who had been on shift were safe, but these four men went down to save the horses. The manager was in front, the under manager behind him, the official of the mine was behind him, with his dog. Now being a warm blooded animal - possibly just like the canary - if the dog had been in front and they had seen him fall down, they would have come out alive.

The manager's last words to my father were, 'You stay here Frank, you guard this post until we come back.'

Well, the next man to go down was a Mr Jenkins. He found my dad unconscious and dragged him into fresh air and when he came round a bit, he left him and found the three men and the dog dead. So my dad having qualified as an undermanager worked in that position from 1915 until his retirement. He saw many managers come and go and he knew all the families of everyone employed here.

He fought that underground fire for four months until it was satisfactorily extinguished.

Colin commented, "They say that you can't smell methane but you are always aware of something. The miner is much safer today, for there is a great booster fan that can blow your hat off underground. It's like a hurricane sometimes which will dilute and disperse any gasses."

Glyn observed, "Blaenafon Coal was particularly good for raising steam. Everybody wanted Welsh steam coal because it was the best in the world. Today's power stations are not so fussy because they are very efficient. They can burn anything now, with the result that foreign rubbish gets imported, but when you burn it on your home fire, it's very smokey."

"The last seam worked at Big Pit," commented Graham, "was the Garw - 2 ft. 3 in. seam. It was a narrow place to work, but the conditions were good,

with a rock top and a rock floor. I got used to working the Garw seam and in the end I didn't even mind crawling 200 yards to reach the Garw face."

Colin interjected, "But when you take people down the mine and show them where you used to work, just looking at it makes them want to turn around and run out."

Graham laughed and said, "I met a lady here this week, who had come home to Wales from Australia after fifty years. Her uncle was Dick Gaut. He was a little bandy-legged man who was less than five feet high, very broad and a character all on his own. He would walk hardly bending into his headings for they were only a bit under his height and they were known as Gaut's Headings."

Glyn added, "All parts of the mine were named after the men who had worked in that particular area, and also the equipment. Take, for example Cowboy's Crosscut. This particular character was given that nickname because one day he was on Brynmawr Square, wearing a stetson hat. He stood in front of a double decker bus with a Mackeson bottle in each hand. He pointed them at the bus and shouted to the driver, 'Throw down the strong box.'

From that time onwards, the Crosscut he was operating in work was known as Cowboy's Crosscut."

Graham smiled and said, "Yes, most people had a nick name and in the old days they were even transferred from father to son. When the father finished or died, the son would take the nick name over."

"There was nothing like working underground for the comradeship was great," said Colin. "I have never known such a fabulous bunch of chaps. You would work together underground, come up, have a bath together, enjoy a cup of tea and a chat in the canteen together, and then go home on the bus together. In the evening you would even go out and have a few beers together. On the weekends the wives would also get together. Yes it was really great.

But as the pits closed and people travelled further to work, we would still enjoy the camaraderie down the pit, but when you went home, you went in different directions. It wasn't the same and the mining communities broke up in that way."

"Any pit was just the same - with a fabulous bunch of blokes working there," said Glyn. "But once they burn the four legs off the pithead gear and collapse it, the mine has gone forever. Gone also is the work and the comradeship. A friend of mine worked at Taff Merthyr and when it closed he got a job in a crisp factory - but in no way was the comradeship like it was underground."

"It was hard work making the transition from miner to museum guide," laughed Colin. "Well, with some of the visitors anyway. But we are doing something that we know a lot about. We certainly still get some good laughs underground, with some of the questions that people ask you. I found it nerve racking at first, with fifteen or sixteen people around you. It's like show business. You are on the stage all the time - until the tour is finished and then you start again with another group.

We often get asked, 'Where did you get trained for this job?' Well, we've had training in safety matters of course, but none of us have trained to be guides. We just take the parties down and tell them what they want to know about mining and about our personal experiences."

Glyn added, "We get people from all over the world and we have guides here who have learned quite a lot of French since they started, because we have to deal with quite a few French people. Sometimes they can't speak a word of English. So all the things underground - the drams, ropes, picks, shovels, roadways etc.. we refer to in French.

Fifty-seven years of age and one is learning French. There aren't many miners who can say that! People who come here are quite impressed that we speak French - with a Welsh accent of course!

I once had a lady say to me, 'Tell me, I have heard that you used to keep a bird in the mine - is it true?' Well, obviously she was referring to the canary, which was used for detecting gas. She asked, 'Was it a parrot?' No, I replied, it wasn't a parrot, it was a canary. The only miner who would use a parrot would be one who'd lost a leg!"

Blaenafon Coal

Coal mined at Blaenafon had special qualities. In particular it had great steam raising power with low ash and an unusually low percentage of sulphur. The latter prevented clinkering on the bars of iron thus saving labour and waste. Owing to its binding properties there was a complete absence of sparking which was a quality of high importance with railways operating in hot countries.

In the early years of the 20th century Blaenafon was producing 500,000 tons of coal a year. It was originally used in the iron furnaces and also supplied neighbouring towns with household fuel, but in later years it was in great demand for powering steamships and railway locomotives. The two pioneer railways of England, the London & North Western and the Great Western were both regular buyers. The first railway system in France, the Chemin de fer de L'Ouest used Blaenafon coal and it was also shipped to South America for consumption on their railways.

By 1873 the Blaenafon Iron and Coal Company was operating sixteen collieries, but by 1906 only six were still working. These were Big Pit, Kay's Slope, Dodd's, Forge, Tunnel Level and Milfraen Pit. In 1925 there were 2,954 men working in the Blaenafon collieries but by 1938, Big Pit, Kay's Slope and Garn Drift (opened in 1930) were the only collieries still working and in 1932 the number of miners employed had been reduced to 1,900. Kay's Slope and Garn closed in 1958.

Big Pit

Big Pit at Blaenafon is one of the oldest shaft mines in the South Wales Coalfield. It was sunk in 1860 and is so named because of its unusually wide shaft which measures 6 metres across. It was the first shaft in the area that was large enough to wind two trams of coal side by side. Ventilation was secured by means of a Waddle fan and this colliery possessed an advantage which is unusual in the Welsh coalfields, of being so free of gas that open lights could be used in the workings.

The mine was kept clear of water by two pumps, a Cameron pump with two inverted cylinders and two 6 inch single acting rams, which forced the water from the workings to the bottom of the pit, where another pump raised it 50 yards up the shaft to an adit through which it ran off by gravity.

The comparatively shallow depth at which the seams lie, the freedom of gas, the paucity of water, accompanied by good roofs and thick seams gave the Blaenafon Company great advantages in the safe and economical working of their immense area. Five seams in Big Pit were worked by the longwall system and the sixth, the Elled seam was worked by the pillar and stall method. The last coal face in production was 2.5 km from the pit bottom.

There were four haulage engines supplied with steam from four Cornish boilers and the winding engines, which are still in use are a pair of 26 inch horizontal cylinders, raising two loaded trams per journey.

Big Pit had a very good safety record and its only major disaster was the incident referred to by Graham Gratton in 1913 when a fire swept through the mine. It was evacuated and all the men on the night shift were brought to the surface safely. A party of volunteers was then sent down to examine the damage. But as they were lowered into the pit they were enveloped by gas and three men were killed. It was nine hours before their bodies could be recovered.

By 1958 Big Pit was employing more than 1,000 men but by 1970 the number had been reduced to just 494 and only the 2 ft. 6 in. Garw seam was being worked.

The manpower dropped to 250 by 1979 and the mine finally closed on 2 February. The seams were too thin and it was difficult to extract the remaining coal.

The 76 remaining miners were transferred to neighbouring collieries and the lower levels of Big Pit, 500 feet down, were allowed to fill up with water. But plans were immediately put into operation to preserve the mine as a living memorial to the Welsh coal industry. More than 100,000 visitors come to Big Pit every year, to descend the 294 metres shaft in the cage, to experience the realm of the collier and see the upper seams where the coal is still exposed.

Big Pit is open daily from the beginning of March to the end of November and underground tours take place between 10.00 am and 3.30 pm.

Cwmbyrgwm Balance Pit

On the hillside above Abersychan, off the B4246 (SO 326204) can be seen the remains of the Cwmbyrgwm water-balance headgear. A shaft was sunk here in about 1820 and the mine supplied the British Ironworks with coal.

A water-balance lift was used to raise coal from the bottom of the mineshaft to the surface. In principle it was a similar system to the Water Balance Tower at Blaenafon Ironworks. A container resting at the bottom of the shaft was filled with coal while at the top of the shaft was an empty container. This was filled with water and being heavier than the coal container, it descended the shaft, pulling the coal up at the same time. The coal was then unloaded at the top of the shaft and the water run out of the container. The process was then repeated.

Elliot Colliery (New Tredegar)

This colliery and the nearby settlement of Elliotstown near New Tredegar, were named after Sir George Elliot, a Geordie coal miner who became a director of the Powell Duffryn Company. This colliery worked coking and steam coal. It closed in 1967. Preserved on the site of the East Pit is a stone engine house built in 1891. Inside is a twin tandem compound winding engine and it is the last example to be seen in South Wales, being preserved here as an industrial monument. It is situated off the A4049 to the south of New Tredegar town centre (SO 144028).

Left: *Cwmbyrgwm water-balance headgear before being dismantled. It was used to raise coal from the bottom of the mine shaft to the surface.*

Right: *At Glyn Pits near Pontypool can be seen the remains of this pumping engine house containing a Cornish-type beam engine with the beam and seventeen-foot wheel still in situ.*

Glyn Pits

This colliery was originally owned by the Hanbury family and it was one of the first to be sunk in this area. The sinking was carried out by Capel Hanbury Leigh around 1840-5 and on one of the two stone buildings that remains on the site can be seen a plaque inscribed 'CHL (Capel Hanbury Leigh) 1845'. The two stone engine houses both still contain their engines which were made at the Neath Abbey works in 1845. This was one of the first coal mines in South Wales to use steam.

Inside the pumping engine house is a Cornish-type beam engine with the beam and the seventeen-foot wheel still in situ. The engine is a double acting single cylinder, 24 in. bore and 6 ft. stroke. It operated at 50 lbs pressure and pumping was carried out in two stages giving a delivery of 9,000 to 12,000 gallons per hour. The shaft depth is 186 metres and the pump delivered into a water course 85 metres from the surface. The water flowed through an underground roadway to a lower surface level in the valley by gravity.

The vertical steam engine in the other stone building was in use until 1932, although the last recorded date of working coal here is 1928. Winding was carried out in two shafts at the same time and the engine is cased between four elegant fluted Doric columns. High above are the winding wheels, each 15 ft. in diameter.

In 1855 the Glyn Pits were acquired by the Ebbw Vale Company. When the company was re-formed in 1891 as the Ebbw Vale Steel, Iron & Coal Co. Ltd., they sub-let their Pontypool mineral estate, including the Glyn Pits to James and William Wood, Colliery proprietors of Glasgow.

The last recorded date of the colliery working is 1928 when it was owned by the Crumlin Valley Collieries Ltd., Pontypool, who also owned Hafodyrynys Colliery. It stopped operation in 1932 but was later used as a pumping station for Hafodyrynys Colliery. Modern pumping equipment was used instead of the old beam engine and was in operation until 1966 when the NCB stopped pumping at Glyn Pits. The shafts were filled in but the two engine houses and their machinery were left intact for preservation and future restoration.

In Trevethin Church, near Pontypool, is a beautiful memorial window which was formally unveiled by Mr. J.C. Hanbury on November 3, 1890.

An inscription on it reads:

'To the Glory of God and in affectionate Memory of 181 Colliers of whom 5 lost their lives in the Glyn Pit on 23rd January 1890, and 176 perished in the disaster at the Llanerch Pit on 6th February, 1890. Erected by the Pontypool Fire Brigade, Gus Bevan, Capt. Nov 3rd 1890.'

Llanerch Colliery

Situated in the parish of Trevethin about 3 miles north of Pontypool, the Llanerch Colliery was sunk by the Ebbw Vale Co in 1858 and was originally known as Cwmnantddu until it was leased to Partridge, Jones & Co Ltd., in January 1887.

It consisted of two shafts 253 yards deep. (Up cast 16 ft by 11 ft. and down cast 13 ft. in diameter). The main seam worked here was the 'Meadow Vein' which was 7 ft. 6 in. thick and worked by the pillar and stall sytem. It produced an annual output of over 7,000 tons.

Ventilation of this colliery was by means of a furnace, until October 1888, when a Walker's patent fan was introduced. The air to ventilate the workings went down to the face of 'Cook's Slope' and was prevented from entering the headings by means of doors placed at the entrances. Having reached the extreme end of the slope, the air returned by the road which is parallel with 'Cook's Slope', and was made to traverse each working place off the headings by means of doors and sheets.

On Thursday 6 February 1890 an explosion took place in Cook's Slope in which 176 men and boys lost their lives.

Risca Colliery

In 1811 the three sons of William Johnson commenced the working of levels in the Black Vein Wood which they later sold to John Russell in 1837. He sank a pit in the same year which reached the thick coal seam known as the Black Vein at a depth of 120 yards. By 1841 this colliery was one of the largest in this part of the coalfield, employing 315 men.

An explosion in the Risca Pit in 1861 killed 232 men. There were 50 married men among the victims. They left 119 children fatherless behind them. There were 63 men who were below that survived. One grief-stricken

woman waited 14 days and nights at the pit-head until the body of her husband was brought to the surface. On 15 July 1880 at 1.30 a.m. an explosion killed another 120 men and boys.

In 1918 there was a serious fire at the Black Vein when casualties were averted by the bravery of a number of workmen and company officials who went down the pit and extinguished the spreading fire. The Risca miners presented them with a certificate of honour which read:

'This is a token of grateful appreciation of the manly courage, gallant heroism and ceaseless devotion to duty displayed on the occasion of the memorable 'gob fire' which broke out at Old Black Vein Colliery between July 12 and August 9, 1918.

During that period of great anxiety and peril they entered the mine in the face of great personal danger and worked with wonderful courage, unremitting energy and self-sacrifice in order that the pit might be rendered safe for their fellow workmen to resume their ordinary callings in the getting of coal at the time of the great European War and when there was urgent need for coal to meet the national emergency.

In placing on record this appreciation the workmen feel that such heroic action and self-sacrifice will live as a noble example and inspiration to future generations, and also serve as a reminder that the coalmines produce their great heroes no less than the battlefield.'

Nine Mile Point (also known as Coronation Colliery)

During the sinking of this pit in 1904 a tragic accident occurred which resulted in the loss of seven lives. The shaft in the east pit had been sunk to a depth of 725 yards and the west pit had reached a depth of 170 yards. During the course of the sinking the men had gone through rock, marl and clay. Their hardest borings were over and they expected to have much softer ground to overcome to reach the Black Vein seam.

Seventeen men were at work in the west pit when the accident occurred. The sinkers had walled all the depth to which they had gone with the exception of about 6 yards. About ten minutes before they were due to come up to the surface, a fall occurred from one side of the shaft burying seventeen men. Only one man escaped - by jumping on the bowk (large bucket) which was just going up. He reached the surface and raised the alarm.

The rescuers managed to dig out and save all but seven men when a second fall prevented the recovery of any further miners and the remaining seven had to be left buried.

In October 1935, a new form of strike action was used at this Sirhowy Valley colliery. A party of miners staged the first 'stay in' strike by remaining at their places underground in the colliery workings until their grievances had been settled. They refused to come to the surface and food had to be sent down to them for they remained below for several days. The idea for such strike action originated in America.

Important events relating to the Monmouthshire coal mining industry

1698 Thomas Savery invents a non-reciprocating steam pump.

1712 Thomas Newcomen makes his first steam beam pumping engine at Dudley Castle, Staffordshire - the first practical steam engine.

1763 Newcomen engin is first used for winding coal at Hartley Colliery, Northumberland.

1769 Watt makes his first experimental steam pumping engine at Kinneil.

1799 Combination Act suppressing associations of work men/unions.

1782 Bridge Level opens at Blaenafon.

1806 Cornish boiler is introduced by Trevethick.

1807 Mechanical ventilator is invented by John Buddle.

1815 Invention of the Davy Lamp.

1823 Shipments of coal from Newport 256,795 tons.

1824 Combination Acts repealed.

1830 Export of South Wales coal begins.

1831 First mining union in South Wales is established.

1832 Anti Truck Act passed by Parliament.

1834 New Poor Law.

1835 Parliamentary inquiry into mine disasters.
495,777 tons of coal shipped from Newport.

1836 First deep mine shaft in Monmouthshire is sunk at Abercarn.

1837 21 killed in mining accident at Blaina.
Bailey's Drift Mine, Nantyglo - 5 men 1 boy and 1 girl killed in an explosion.

1838 Cinder Pits Blaenafon 14 men and 2 women are drowned when torrential rain floods pit.

1841 Miners Association of Great Britain and Ireland is formed.

1842 Mines and Collieries Act forbids the employment of girls and boys under 10 years of age in pits.

1843 First Government Inspector of mines is appointed.

1846 Gas explosion at Black Vein Colliery, Risca kills 35 miners.

1847 617,177 tons of coal shipped from Newport.

1848 11 die in an explosion at Victoria Colliery.

1850 First Government Inspector of Mines is appointed with power to go underground.
Black Vein Colliery, Risca - 3 men killed and 8 injured in a pit blast.

1853 Black Vein Colliery, Risca - 10 miners die and the pit is christened 'The Death Pit'.

1855 An Act is passed outlining powers and duties of inspectors.

1857 13 die in underground blast at Cwmtillery Colliery.

1859 Worthington invents his Duplex steam pump.

1860 Act regulating inspection of mines.
Varteg Pit is sunk.
Black Vein Colliery, Risca - 146 die in the worst explosion in British mining history.

1861 British Top Pits sunk.
Black Vein Colliery, Risca - 232 killed in an explosion.

1863 Formation of National Union of Miners.

1865 Blaendare Pit is sunk.
New Bedwellty Pit - 27 are killed in an explosion.

1869 Llanerch Colliery, Pontypool - 7 men killed underground.

1889 Glyn Tillery Pit is sunk.

1872 Coal Mines Regulation Act.
Victoria Colliery - 18 men and 1 boy are killed in an explosion.

1873 Newport Abercarn Black Vein Steam Coal Company Limited is formed with the purpose of sinking the Celynnen (south) Colliery to exploit 'the most valuable coal seam in the United Kingdom'.
Cwmtillery Colliery - 6 are killed in an explosion.

1875 New Tredegar Colliery - 22 are killed in a gas explosion.

1876 Prince of Wales Colliery, Abercarn - 3 killed.
Explosion at Cwmtillery Colliery kills 18 men.

1878 Prince of Wales Colliery, Abercarn - 268 men and boys are killed in an explosion.

1879 Bedwellty Pit, Tredegar - 3 men are killed.
Waun Pit, Cwmavon - 6 men and 1 boy fall to their deaths when a broke breaks as a cage is lowered.
Waunllwyd Colliery, Ebbw Vale - 84 miners are killed.

1880 Risca Colliery - 120 men and boys and 69 horses are killed in an explosion.

1887 The Coal Mines Regulation Act.

1889 Miners Federation of Great Britain is formed.

Year	Event
1890	Glyn Pits, Pontypool - 5 men are killed in a fire.
	Llanerch Colliery, Pontypool - explosion kills 176.
1894	Coal Mines Act.
1895	Introduction of electric and compressed air-driven and cutting machines.
1898	South Wales Miners Federation is established.
1900	Gwenallt (Cwmffrwdoer) Pit is sunk.
1902	Milfraen Colliery, Blaenafon - 5 are killed.
	McLaren No.1 Pit, Abertwysswg - an explosion kills 17.
	Tirpentwys Colliery - 8 are killed in shaft accident.
1905	First belt conveyor is introduced in a Yorkshire Colliery.
	Coal Mines Act.
	Six Bells Colliery, Abertillery - 1 man is killed in an explosion.
	Nine Mile Point Colliery, Risca - 7 men are killed.
1908	New Coal Mines Regulations are introduced to increase safety in pits.
	Big Pit, Blaenafon - an explosion kills 3 men.
1909	Eight hour day is introduced in the coal industry.
	44,298 colliers are employed in Monmouthshire cutting coal.
	7,175 men are employed above ground attending to engines, coke ovens etc.
1910	Britannia Colliery, Monmouthshire becomes the first all electric colliery in Britain.
	British New Pit, Talywain is sunk.
1911	Coal Mines Act.
	Mynydd Maen Pit is sunk.
	Crumlin Valley Pit is sunk.
1912	National miners strike for a minimum wage.
	Minimum Wage Act.
	Markham Navigation Colliery - six men are killed in an explosion whilst sinking a shaft.
	Pengam Colliery, Blackwood - 4 are men killed.
1913	National output of coal: 287.4 million tons.
	Peak year for coal production from South Wales coalfield (57 million tons).
1915	Celynen (North) is sunk.
1921	Coal Mines dispute - National Strike involving 1,100,000 men on strike for 3 months.
1923	Workmens' Compensation Act.
1925	Workmens' Compensation Act.
1926	Mining Industry Act.
	General Strike: 1,075,000 miners go on strike for 9 months.
	They are eventually forced back to work on lower wages than before.
1927	Marine Colliery, Cwm - 52 are killed in gas explosion.
1930	Coal Mines Act.
	Stay down strike at Nine Mile Point Colliery, Risca.
1931	Mining Industry Act.
1932	Bryn Coal Level, Talywain is opened.
1935	Risca Colliery - 186 miners in stay down strike.
1938	Coal Act.
1943	Workmens' Compensation Act.
	Establishment of National Coal Board.
1944 | 112,000 miners are working in the South Wales Coalfield.
1946 | Coal Industry Nationalisation Act.
1947 | Nationalisation of Coal Mines.
1947 | Coal industry is nationalised.
1952 | 31,000 men are employed as miners in Monmouthshire.
1954 | The Mines and Quarries Act.
1960 | Six Bells Colliery - 45 men are killed in an underground explosion.
1966 | Aberfan disaster: 144 people are killed including 116 children when a tip slides down on houses and Infant and Junior schools.
1969 | Mines and Quarries Act.
1971 | 11,400 men are employed as miners in Monmouthshire.
1972 | Seven week national strike over pay.
1974 | Month-long national pay strike and Edward Heath loses a general election called during strike.
1980 | Big Pit, Blaenafon closes and becomes a working museum.
1984/85 | Year-long pit strike follows election of Arthur Scargill as president of the NUM.
1986 | Marine Colliery - the last pit in the county is closed.
1987 | NCB changed to British Coal.
1988 | Cecil Parkinson announces privatisation plan.
1990 | British Coal announces closure of three-fifths of remaining 50 pits.
1992 | Government closure programme kills off all but one of the remaining South Wales pits.
1994 | Completion of sales of pits.

A PASSION FOR STEAM

Steam as a means of power is said to have been thought of by the Greeks, but it was Thomas Newcomen who was really successful in designing a steam engine, which although stationary, had the power to move heavy loads. In 1705 he constructed what was called the atmospheric engine and it was used for pumping water out of a colliery near Wolverhampton.

Fifty years later James Watt came across Newcomen's strange contraption, perfected a condenser to make it work better and patented a fairly successful steam engine - still stationary in 1769. Five years later Watt joined with Boulton, and the famous firm of Watt & Boulton was formed. They were the principal makers of steam engines until the turn of the century, providing power for operating pumps and winding gear.

An eventful year in the history of railways was 1804 when Richard Trevethick, a Cornish engineer, constructed a steam engine which on 20 February ran on rails along the Pen y Darren Tramroad between Merthyr and Abercynon. Samuel Homfray bet rival ironmaster Richard Crawshay 1,000 guineas that a load of ten tons of bar iron could be conveyed along a tramroad from his works to the Navigation Wharf at Abercynon, 9 miles away. Trevethick's locomotive, pulling five waggons loaded with ten tons of freight and carrying seventy men completed this historic journey at an average speed of 6 miles per hour.

In those early years of the nineteenth century there were many far-seeing young engineers who fervently believed in the steam locomotive. William Hedley at Wylam Colliery built his famous 'Puffing Billy' in 1813, but the engineer who is best remembered for his achievements was George Stephenson. Fascinated by the opportunities that seemed possible with a moving steam engine he set to work to improve on Richard Trevethick's designs. By 1814 he had built the 'Blucher' which, though only a year later than the 'Puffing Billy,' was much more successful.

In 1823 work began on the construction of the Stockton and Darlington railway in County Durham. The grand opening took place on September 27th of that year and Stephenson's 'Locomotion No. 1', with an advance guard of a signalman carrying a red flag set off down the line. It pulled a total of thirty-five trucks with a gross load of ninety tons and sped down the iron rails at varying speeds of between 10 and 15 miles an hour. This railway was used for a number of years, transporting coal, but the days of the passenger service had yet to arrive.

It is interesting that during this time there was tremendous opposition to railways, in particular from the canal owners who quickly realised that their canals would go into decline. It was also claimed that the peace of the countryside would be ruined, cattle would be poisoned by the foul smoke, crops damaged and hayricks set on fire by sparks from the noisy engines.

The famous Rainhill trials were held in 1829 with a prize offered for the best locomotive. It was George Stephenson's 'Rocket' which outstripped all the other entrants and became the most renowned locomotive in the world. It weighed just over 4 tons, had two cylinders 8 in. by 7 in., hauled 13 tons at an average speed of just under 14 miles per hour, and actually could reach a maximum speed of just over 30 miles an hour. The name of Stephenson was firmly established and the 'Railway Age' had begun.

The golden age of the railway was the decade between 1840 and 1850 when bills were presented in Parliament for the construction of all sorts of lines. In 1840 the railway mileage in Britain stood at 1,331 miles, but ten years later it had reached 6,635 miles.

During the 1850s there were several important inventions. In 1856 Saxby invented interlocking, which is a safety precaution that locks points and signals at the same time. Ramsbottom, in 1859, designed a successful water-scoop and in that year Mr. Pullman drew up his first plans for sleeping cars in America.

In 1873 the Great Western Railway began to construct the Severn Tunnel which was a tremendous undertaking, and in 1877 it built its first sleeping cars. Also in that year the last sections of broad gauge rails were laid in Britain and conversion to the universal narrow gauge was begun.

With the arrival of the twentieth century, railway mileage in this country stood at 18,672 miles and

Britain's name in the world of engineering and locomotive performance was second to none. In 1923 one hundred and twenty-three separate British companies amalgamated to form what was known as the Big Four, namely, the Southern Railway, the London Midland and Scottish, the London & North Eastern Railway, and the Great Western Railway. The British Railways were nationalised in 1948 and the Big Four and their subsidiary companies were divided into six regions under state control.

Nationalisation was followed by extensive reorganisation in order to meet the competition of road transport. Diesel engines replaced steam locomotives, all valley branch lines were closed and trains ceased to call at intermediate stops on the main lines.

About fifty stations and halts in the valleys of Monmouthshire were closed during 1962-63 and December 1963 saw the end of the rail link between Newport and Brecon. The last branch line in the county ended its eventful history on 13 June 1964, when the last passenger train ran from Pontypool Road, over the famous Crumlin Viaduct to Aberdare and the Vale of Neath. The viaduct was demolished the following year. The County was now left with just five railway stations.

THE CONSTRUCTION OF RAILWAYS
—— IN MONMOUTHSHIRE ——

The majority of railways in Wales were built in the two decades from 1850 to 1870. They were built by small companies in competition with one another and the contractors were local men. Railway construction led to an ever-increasing demand for iron, with the result that in the 1850s there were one hundred and sixty-five furnaces in blast in Wales, prducing a million tons of pig iron. The total for the whole country at that time was just under 4 million tons.

A number of railway schemes were proposed but never constructed. For example in 1842 a proposal was put forward for a railway to run from Newport through High Cross, Henllys, Cwmbran, Pontypool and Pontnewynydd, then by tunnel through Llanhilleth Mountain to Blaina and Nantyglo.

All the Monmouthshire tramroads were gradually converted to railways with the exception of Rassau, Cwmffrwd and Blaendare whose steep gradients were unsuitable for locomotive engines and horse drawn trams continued to be used.

At one time it was rightly said that 'perhaps no county in the kingdom is better off for railway communication than Monmouthshire.'

Newport, Abergavenny & Hereford Railway ———
In 1845 the Newport, Abergavenny & Hereford Railway Company was formed under a special Act of Parliament to construct a steam railway between Pontypool and Hereford. At this time there were three tramroad companies operating between Abergavenny and Hereford. These were the Llanfihangel Co., the Grosmont Co., and the Hereford Co., and they were purchased in 1846.

It would seem that these tramroads were operated by the NA&H Company whilst its new railway of standard gauge was being erected alongside the existing route, with diversions of a few hundred yards on certain sections.

The new railway, together with Abergavenny's first station, was opened on 2 January 1854. Six years later on 1 July the Company was taken over by the West Midland Co., who in turn were swallowed up by the GWR on 1 August 1865.

From Penpergwm, just below Abergavenny where the line crosses the River Usk, the line begins a long ascent. The gradient steepens beyond Abergavenny to 1 in 82 which eases to 1 in 95 before reaching Llanfihangel. A banker (an assisting engine at the rear of a train) was needed by the heaviest trains on this section and one was always kept in readiness at the GWR station.

At one time the old market town of Abergavenny was a very important railway centre with three stations: the **Great Western** on the north to west main line, situated to the south west of the town centre; **Brecon Road**, on the former L & NWR Abergavenny to Merthyr line, and **Abergavenny Junction** at the point where the two lines met, north east of the town. Only the Monmouth Road Great Western Railway station has survived.

Opposite: *'Tornado' Britannia Class locomotive.*

Above: *Castle Class Locomtive*
'Lockheed Hudson' at Abergavenny,
Monmouth Road.

128

Above: *Castle Class Locomotive storming Llanfihangel summit near Abergavenny.*

The Merthyr, Tredegar & Abergavenny Railway ——

This was one of the most spectacular railways in Britain, but it was also one of the most expensive to operate for the long and steep gradients caused coal to be consumed at the rate of 90 lbs per mile.,

Its construction took nineteen years and it was begun on 16 April 1860, when the contract for building the section from Brynmawr to Merthyr was let to Eckersley at a cost of £6,000 per mile. The firm appointed John Gardner as their Engineer.

William McCormick & Co. built the Abergavenny to Nantybwch stretch in two contracts which were let on 8 May 1860 for £84,000 and £101,000. This firm was also responsible for various station works on the line.

Opening Dates
1862 Abergavenny to Brynmawr section opened on 29 September.
1864 Brynmawr to Nantybwch section opened on 1 March.
1871 Nantybwch to Rhymney Bridge section opened on 5 September.
1873 Rhymney Bridge to Dowlais section opened on 1 January.
1879 Penywern Junction to Morlais Junction section opened on 1 January.

Trains departed from Abergavenny Junction and crossed the River Usk on an iron girder bridge. The line then turned sharply to the west and commenced an eight mile ascent to Brynmawr, climbing to a height of 1,160 feet above sea level. This was one of the most severely graded railways in the British Isles with a three mile section of 1 in 34.

From Brynmawr there were branches to Abersychan and Nantyglo while the main line continued over undulating gradients to its terminus at Merthyr Tydfil, 25 miles from Abergavenny Junction.

The section through the Clydach Gorge was particularly dramatic with the line twisting and turning but climbing steadily along the steep slopes above the deep gorge. Its construction was a remarkable engineering achievement and if the line was still in operation today it would be a popular tourist attraction.

Clydach Station was at the end of a sharply curved viaduct 100 yards long and beyond it the trains passed through a 300 yard tunnel. The line passed through a second tunnel at Gelli Felin which was 350 yards in length. On the other side was Gelli Felin Halt which was opened by the LMS on 6 September 1933.

When the trains reached Brynmawr Station the locomotives, having climbed 1,000 feet, took on additional water. This station after all served the highest town in Wales.

Trains descending the Clydach Gorge from Brynmawr took it steady, not exceeding 25 mph and freight trains were restricted to 20 mph. It was necessary for them to travel down this 1 in 37 to 1 in 46 gradient with their brakes constantly applied. However, when they reached the floor of the valley the drivers had to accelerate in order to cope with the gradient leading from the river bridge to Brecon Road Station.

On Tuesdays the trains were always packed with passengers for this is market day in Abergavenny. Most of the people who lived in farms and small-holdings close to the line, used the train to bring their produce for sale in the market. Generally on Tuesdays the Company had to put at least one additional train on the line to accomodate the market day travellers.

To travel beyond Brynmawr on this line in the winter could often be a worrying undertaking, for snow at such an altitude could bring considerable problems. At Christmas in 1927 there were at least fourteen locomotives snowbound at various points along the line between Brynmawr and Merthyr. Forty passengers on one of these trains were marooned at Nantybwch, 1,165 feet above sea level, for twelve hours!

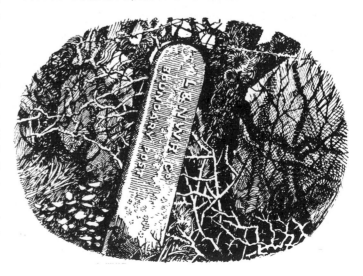

Right: *Railway boundary marker at Clydach Camp.*

Above: *The locomotive sheds at Brecon Road in the days when Abergavenny was an important railway town. The locos in the drawing are a 2-6-2 LMS Tank and an 0-6-2 Coal Tank.*

Above: *Evening train, Brecon Road, Abergavenny with Blorenge looming in the background.*

132

Above: *Govilon Station in about 1950. This was the first station to be completed on the M.T. & A. Railway, when it first opened between Abergavenny and Brynmawr in 1862.*

Above: *A view of the Clydach Tunnels on the M.T.& A. line passing through the wild and romantic Clydach Gorge. This line had a history of one hundred years which included being taken over by the London & North Western Railway Company in 1866. It was closed by Dr. Beeching in 1958.*

Above: *Clydach Lime Works was established in about 1877 to provide lime for the construction of the M.T. & A. Railway viaduct just below the 'Cuckoo Quarry'. The kilns ceased burning in the 1930s but were used again in the Second World War when there was a high demand for lime for agricultural purposes. Lime was last burnt there in 1955.*

Bottom: *The M.T. & A. Railway viaduct below Clydach Station. It was built on a graceful curve and was supported by eight semi-circular arches, each of 30 ft. span.*

Left: *Llanelly Quarry sidings C. 1920*

Above: *LNWR 0-8-0 'Super D' loco, ubiquitous to the Merthyr, Tredegar & Abergavenny line which passed through Tafarnaubach which is now the route of the Heads of the Valleys*

MONMOUTHSHIRE BRANCH LINES

Newport & Pontypool Railway
In 1852 the 'Old Monmouthshire' line, connecting Newport with Pontypool was opened by the Monmouthshire Railway Company.

Pontypool to Blaenafon Railway
This was built by the Monmouthshire Railway Company as a northern extension of their Newport & Pontypool Railway in 1854. It was built along the route of the old tramroad running from the canal head at Pontnewynydd (1796) to Blaenafon Ironworks.

In 1870 the mineral branches from Pontnewynydd Junction to Cwmffrwdoer and Cwmnantddu were opened. They were short but very steep. On the Cwmffrwdoer branch, the gradient was 1 in 22 and it was 1 in 19 on the Cwmnantddu.

The Monmouthshire Railway & Canal Company (sometimes referred to as 'The Mouse, Rat & Cat Company') also constructed a branch line from Trevethin Junction to Talywaun in 1876/7. From Trevethin it climbed at 1 in 48 in a tight half-circle to pass over the top of both the Cwmffrwdoer and Cwmnantddu Branches and then ran parallel with the Blaenafon line. It involved the construction of the Talywaun Viaduct at a point just over 4 miles north of Pontypool. John Gardner was the Engineer and he built this massive viaduct on a curve across the Ffrwd Valley. It is the largest horse-shoe bend on any railway in England and Wales. The line was opened on 18 September, 1879 and it joined the branch from Brynmawr, built by the L &NWR.

The Brecon & Merthyr Railway
This ran from Newport to Brecon, by way of Bassaleg, Rhiwderin, Machen, Maesycwmmer, and Bargoed, where it entered Glamorgan and continued through the Brecon Beacons via Torpantau where it passed through the highest railway tunnel in the British Isles.

The Brynmawr and Blaenafon
In 1868 the London & North Western Railway Company pushed their line southwards from Brynmawr to Blaenafon. The contractor was Joseph

Firbank and John Gardner was the Chief Engineer. The line was opened on 1 November 1869 and it became known as the 'Bed & Breakfast Line'. It climbed at 1 in 40 for just under two miles to Waunafon, a small station at 1,400 feet above sea level. This had the distinction of being the second highest station on a standard-gauge railway in Britain. Leadhills on the Wanlockhead in Scotland was the highest at 1,498 feet. (The highest point on a main line railway in Britain today is Druimuacddar at 1,484 feet on the main line between Perth and Inverness). Waunafon Station was also situated on the boundary of Monmouthshire and Breconshire. It closed to passengers on 5 May 1941 and closed entirely on 23 June 1954.

The original terminus of the Brynmawr to Blaenafon line was the Blaenafon L & NWR Station which opened in January 1870. In later years the line was extended to join the low level route near Pontypool. This station, the goods warehouse and the engine shed were all neatly placed together on the hillside on the western side of the valley, opposite the town of Blaenafon which rose up the hill on the other side. It was closed to passenger services in 1941 but freight traffic continued until the early 1960s.

Blaenavon to Varteg Line
A mineral branch line 1.5 miles long ran from Blaenafon to Varteg Hill Colliery mostly on a rising gradient of 1 in 45. The rails, which were upside down (in the 1920s) had previously been in the Mersey Tunnel, so they saw service in what were probably the lowest and also one of the highest lengths of railway in Britain.

The Beaufort to Ebbw Vale
This branch Line was opened as a single track railway on 1 Sptember, 1867. The contractors were T. Bressey and W. Field with John Gardner as Engineer. It closed ninety two years later in 1959 when coal traffic from Tredegar came to an end. Beaufort Station was destroyed when the Heads of the Valleys Road was constructed.

Ebbw Valley Railway
The Sirhowy and Ebbw Valley Railways met at Risca. Half a mile south of Cross Keys was Hall's Road

Opposite: Low Level Railway Station at Ebbw Vale was so-named by British Railways in 1950 to distinguish it from the GWR station. A multi-storey car park now stands on this site.

Junction where a mineral line built on Benjamin Hall's Tramroad was leased by the GWR and converted into a railway. Aberbeeg Station lay at the junction of the Ebbw Vale and Brynmawr lines and had four platform faces.

Pontypool, Caerleon and Newport Railway

When proposed in 1865 it was intended that this new railway would incorporate the existing Caerleon Tramroad. However when it was built it did not follow the route of the tramroad all the way. It was completed in 1874.

Brecon & Merthyr Railway

In 1860 the Brecon & Merthyr Railway Company bought up the old Rumney Tramroad and converted it into a railway, obtaining powers to run over the Western Valley lines from Bassaleg into Newport.

Sirhowy Valley Railway

An Act of Parliament in 1860 authorised the conversion of the Sirhowy Tramroad to a standard gauge railway. In the construction of the new line the route of the original tramroad was followed most of the way but some deviations were made.

A public passenger service over this railway was introduced in June 1865 and ten years later the Sirhowy Valley Railway became part of the London & North Western Railway to be later taken over by the London, Midland & Scottish Railway.

The opening of the Sirhowy Valley Railway was described in the Monmouthshire Merlin in 1865:

'Last Monday the Sirhowy Valley Railway was opened for passenger traffic, and the important advantages thereby conferred on the public of the district traversed by the line, may be gathered from the anxiety with which for months the event has been anticipated.

...The object of the Sirhowy Valley Railway is to bring Tredegar and Sirhowy, and adjacent collieries and works, into closer communication with the port of Newport. It is between fourteen and fifteen miles in length, and starting from Sirhowy - which is practically one with Tredegar, the two forming the centre of a considerable population, principally employed at the important and growing works there

conducted - runs through a beautifully wooded and picturesque valley down to Nine-mile Point, where a junction is effected with the Monmouthshire Railway Company's line, over which the Sirhowy have running powers to Newport and into the Dock Street Station. But the route of the Sirhowy has other recommendations than those to be found in its romantic natural scenery; it is opulent in rich mineral seams, and these can hardly fail of being largely developed by the improved railway communication now completed, and in the absence of which many parts of the district now easily reached, have long been difficult of access.'

A section of the line running through Tredegar Park beside the River Ebbw was known as the Golden Mile for a toll was paid to the Morgans of Tredegar House for each truck of coal transported along this route. In 1880 it was recorded that the Park Mile was realising a net profit of £5,000 per annum. Three years later the widening of the Park Mile to take the Pontypridd & Caerphilly Railway was authorised and in that year it was recorded that four million tons of coal passed annually along its lines, producing an income of £10,000.

In 1889 the Monmouthshire County Council pressed for an assessment of the Park Mile and Lord Tredegar subsequently undertook to pay £200 per annum as county and police rates. The GWR bought out the tolls in 1923.

Crumlin Viaduct

The most difficult problem that confronted the railway engineers was on the cross valley line in the southern part of Monmouthshire. A connection was needed for the Aberdare district with that of Pontypool Road. The Taff Vale Extension Line at that time ended at High Level Station, Crumlin which was faced by another terminus on the opposite side of the valley.

T.W. Kennard & Sons were awarded the contract for the construction of the Crumlin Viaduct in 1853. Their first action was to establish a works at the eastern end of the viaduct site. This became known as the 'Nut and Bolt Works' and it remained in operation for a period of fifty eight years. An inclined plane was built to enable ironwork to be taken down to the valley floor.

Preparations were then made to erect the first pier. They drained and excavated the canal near the basin to the north of the viaduct site and laid a foundation at a depth of fourteen feet. It consisted of one foot of concrete, a course of four inch Memel timbers and a twelve foot course of masonry to which the baseplates were bolted.

This part of the structure became known as the Isabella Pier being named after Lady Isabella Fitzmaurice who attended a stone laying ceremony here on 8 December 1853. A casket of new coins was placed in the foundations and she celebrated the erection of the first piece of ironwork by breaking a bottle of wine over it. The watching workmen gave a loud and hearty cheer and one intrepid fellow sauntered across a girder 1 ft. in width and 200 ft. from the ground.

While work was progressing on the viaduct, the Glyn Ponds near Pontypool were drained and a railway line laid along the floor of the valley. It reached Crumlin on 20 August 1855.

The contractor T.W. Kennard had Crumlin Hall built just down the valley in a suitable location for him to be able to watch the progress of his great viaduct from his study window.

Horizontal girders, each 150 ft. in length were fabricated on the floor of the valley and lifted into position by a steam winch. A gang of twenty men were paid in total the sum of £5 per day to prepare each girder for lifting. The first girder was lifted successfully on 3 December 1854, but the next one collapsed and a man riding on it was killed. Subsequent girders were braced with timber until they were secured to the apex of their respective piers and no further accidents occurred. It took a whole day to lift one girder to the highest point of the viaduct, rising above the valley floor at a rate of 4 in. per minute. The last girder was lifted into place on 17 December 1855. Decking was then laid, consisting of 6 inch Memel timbers in 26 feet lengths.

All the iron for the bridge was produced by the Blaenafon Iron Company and the castings were made at the Kennard Works, Falkirk. Boring, turning and fitting was carried out in the 'Nut & Bolt Works' at the Pontypool end of the viaduct. Before the bridge could be opened it had to be tested in the presence of Colonel Wynne the Board of Trade Inspector. The London and North Western Railway provided six tank engines which were coupled together with a waggon load of pig iron, making a total weight of 380 tons. A volunteer driver had to be found with the necessary courage to make the crossing. 'Mad Jack' from Pontypool came forward and he was instructed to drive the train at crawling speed across the bridge to avoid exposing it to any early or unnatural strains. Apparently before making the crossing he went into the village of Crumlin and visiting every pub, he drank large quantities of beer to give him the necessary courage. When at last he felt up to the task in hand, he got into his engine and set off with a roar, and hurtled towards the viaduct which he crossed at great speed. Reproached by the whitefaced engineer afterwards, he explained, 'When eternity looks you straight in the face, you may as well go full speed to meet it!' This escapade apparently did no harm to the structure and the contractor T.W. Kennard, sat down to a celebration dinner that night accompanied by 150 guests. He must have been a very satisfied man for his huge viaduct was at last finished. He knew that the job had been well done and that it would last for at least a hundred years.

An opening ceremony was held on Whit Monday 1857. It was a grand occasion which attracted a large crowd, the majority of which were labourers with their wives and children. Beer booths were set up in the fields and the viaduct was draped with flags from top to bottom. As a tribute to the contractor a floral archway was set up bearing the words 'Long life and prosperity to T.W. Kennard.' Guns were fired throughout the day and gaily decorated trains arrived from different parts of Britain.

Two ballad singers had composed a song about the building of the viaduct and they walked around singing their heads off and selling their verses for a penny a sheet. It had the following chorous:-

'Thousands have come from far and near
So full of youth and bloom
To open the Great Crumlin bridge
On the glorious First of June.'

It certainly was a great bridge, for not only was it the longest railway bridge in the world but the highest in

Britain and the third highest in the world. Also it was the least expensive bridge for its size that had ever been constructed.

The August 1857 edition of the *Illustrated London News* described it as *'a wonderful structure more remarkable as a combination of lightness and economy of material, than it is for boldness of design and beauty of execution. The Crumlin Viaduct with the exception of the Aqueduct of Spoletto and the Portage Timber viaduct in the United States exceeds any other structure of the kind in height. It is a remarkable example of the modern application of iron to such a purpose.'*

The bridge was 1,658 ft. long and 208 ft. high from the valley floor to the top of the handrails. It was built by 200 men in four and a half years. The materials in its construction included 2,500 tons of iron, 30,000 cubic ft. of timber and 11,000 cubic ft. of ashlar masonry. The total cost was £62,000. Fifteen tons of paint were used to protect the metalwork and it was repainted by contractors at intervals of five to seven years.

By passing through a trapdoor at each end of the structure one could walk the entire length of the viaduct and gain an insight into the quantity and size of the bolts and ironwork involved in its construction. The view from this walkway was described by a Pontypool man who walked it in 1875:-

'I and my companion were anxious to get to the top and we luckily met a couple of good fellows who kindly accompanied us as guides. We smoked a pipe along the footroad under the rails, and then over the rails. There was a delightful view of the beautiful valley enclosed in luxuriantly wooded heights, the village of Newbridge, Crumlin Hall crowning the ridge on the right and beneath us the River Ebbw, the canal, the village of Crumlin, the railway from Newport to Aberbeeg junction and the works at which the viaduct was built.'

A travel writer came to Crumlin thirteen years after the viaduct was built and described it with obvious enthusiasm:-

'From east to west, high above the lovely valley, high above the nestling houses and the glittering waters, stretches the lace like viaduct, light and delicate as if it were the work of the fairy Ariel. So light does it appear, that even now, though it has stood the severest tests, and has been a thing established for thirteen years, many people are still too timorous to cross it.

The viaduct owes its origin to the genius of the late T.W. Kennard Esq., but it is only one of many glories of art that will perpetuate his memory and that of his sons. Emanating from the works carried out by Messrs Kennard Brothers, immediately under the viaduct; many other bridges of this class have been sent to remote parts of the world.

They are seen on the Barrukar and several railways in India, the Murray river in Australia, the Pernambuco Railway in South America and the Tagus and other rivers and railways in Spain, Portugal, the Tiber and the Vollatri Valley near Rome.

If you should ever land on the pier at Wellington, New Zealand, you will set foot on the work of Messrs Kennard Brothers, made at Crumlin.'

Over the years an average of six passenger trains daily ran each way between Pontypool and Neath, with connections for Swansea. The motive power was provided by the Pontypool Road and Aberdare sheds. Much of the coal from the Glamorgan coal fields on the Taff Vale extension went across the viaduct, and during the 1914 - 18 war, it carried as many as sixteen trains a day of Admiralty coal. They were heading for destinations in the north, and added stresses far beyond those for which the bridge had been designed.

During the 1930s there was concern over the possibility of the viaduct's stability being affected by mining subsidence. As a result the bridge section was converted to single line, the track being placed in the centre of the structure and an electric train token system was installed between Crumlin Junction and Crumlin Station (High Level).

The last scheduled passenger train to cross the viaduct was the 9.10 p.m. from Neath to Pontypool Road on Saturday 13 June 1964. During the following year the now disused viaduct was used as a set for the film 'Arabesque' which included a sequence that showed Gregory Peck and Sophia Loren running along the walkway and being dive bombed by a helicopter.

In 1962 the viaduct had been scheduled by the Ministry of Housing and Local Government as being of

architectural and historic interest, but British Railways decided that the demolition of the mighty structure was the best course of action. It was estimated that the metal in the bridge based on a scrap value of £15 per ton would bring in £38,250.

Demolition was carried out by Messrs Birds of Swansea who specialised in tearing down steelworks, various industrial undertakings and bridges that have had their day. The work was programmed to take 9 months and was supervised by Brian Houston Barron. His biggest problem was the wind which at times proved very troublesome.

The ten man demolition team began by choosing a 150 ft. experimental section on the east side of the viaduct. They first took up the railway lines on that section, removed the sleepers and the ballast, and cut the deck-plates. Then down came the girders. A crane on the ground was needed, capable of lifting 100 tons and equipped with a 200 ft. long jib. Two other cranes each able to lift a 37 ton load were positioned on either side of the working sector of the bridge. Protected by safety harnesses, the demolition team methodically made progress and piece by piece dismantled the eight piers which supported the bridge. It was a difficult and dangerous operation, but they completed the job in June 1966 and the great Crumlin Viaduct became just a memory.

An official report compiled by the British Railways Chief Civil Engineer stated that:-

'While the structure was undoubtedly of great engineering and historic interest, it was nearing the end of its useful life as a railway viaduct. Even with heavy expenditure on maintenance the viaduct could not be expected to have a life of more than about twenty years without involving a serious risk to public safety.'

Many local people had opposed the demolition and one Abertillery Councillor who had fought hard to save it afterwards commented; 'I think time will show that the destruction of the viaduct was not only a species of vandalism brought about because the achievements of the pioneers of progress are not appreciated, but a blunder as well.'

Coleford, Monmouth, Usk & Pontypool Railway ——
The Coleford, Monmouth, Usk & Pontypool Railway

was incorporated on 20 August 1853 as a single line railway from the Newport, Abergavenny & Hereford Railway at Little Mill Junction to Wyesham. The 15 mile section from Little Mill to Monmouth (Troy) was opened on 2 June 1856 and extended to Wyesham by 1 July, 1861.

The purpose of this railway was to carry iron ore from the Forest of Dean to the Nantyglo furnaces, pit wood for use in the collieries and farm produce for workers in the industrial valleys. It closed on 30 May, 1955. Most of the route from Usk to Monmouth has been made into the A40/A449 road. The tunnel at Usk can still be seen just east of the old station. (SO 421075).

The Wye Valley Railway ————————————
The Wye Valley Railway was authorised on 10 August 1866 and construction of the 13 mile line between Wye Valley Junction on the South Wales main line, east of Chepstow, and Wyesham Halt, Monmouth, commenced in May 1874. It took two years to build this line and the cost was just over £300,000. The scheme involved the excavation of a 1,188 yards tunnel beneath Tidenham, a 700 yard tunnel near Tintern and the construction of three bridges across the River Wye. The line was opened on 1 November 1876.

Pursuing a sinuous course the single track kept close to the river for most of the way, crossing it several times and providing impressive views. The journey from Chepstow to Monmouth took about 50 minutes, during which the train stopped twelve times at:- Netherhope, Tidenham, Tintern, Brockweir, Bigsweir (later re-named St. Briavel's Halt), Whitebrook, Penallt, Redbrook and Wyesham. It was only at Tintern Station that two trains were able to pass one another.

The locomotives originally used on this line were mainly of the 517 light tank class. They had burnished brass domes, round-eyed windows and copper capped chimneys, and were manufactured in Wolverhampton during the period 1868 to 1885. On 1 July 1905 the Wye Valley Railway was amalgamated with the Great Western Railway.

Two pannier tank engines numbers 6412 and 6439 pulled the last passenger train consisting of 8 coaches on the final journey from Monmouth to Chepstow on 4 January 1959. The line was used for goods traffic until 6 January 1964.

In 1970 the site was purchased by Monmouthshire County Council. Subsequently the very overgrown site was cleared and developed by Gwent County Council into a very pleasant picnic area now known as 'The Old Station, Tintern'. The main building and the signal box were carefully restored and now respectively serve as refreshment and exhibition rooms. There are also two restored carriages which have been brought to the site. One of them is an ex-British Rail Eastern Region vehicle built in 1955 as a brake van bogie. Painted in BR maroon it houses an exhibition which tells the story of the Wye Valley Railway and provides lecture facilities for visiting parties. The other carriage is a GWR coach built in 1935. It is used as an information and sales area. There is also a 'Pooley Van' exhibited here. This was a mobile forge and workshop which could be summoned to anywhere on the system where a weighing machine needed attention.

Gwent County Council won a Civic Trust Award in 1978 for the sympathetic restoration of these old railway buildings and at the time it was commented: 'Lucky are the tourists who discover this delightful place which so skilfully evokes the vanished beauty of the remarkable Wye Valley Railway.' The Old Station is on the route of the Wye Valley Walk and there are also several short waymarked walks leading from the site.

A miniature steam train is operated on the site by members of the Newport Model Engineering Society providing rides for youngsters on Bank Holidays and on the last Sunday of every month from Easter until the end of October. One of the locomotoves regularly used is Cyril Goulding's 1400 Class Tank Engine, a scale model of one which ran on the line years ago.

MEMORIES OF WORKING AT TINTERN STATION

In 1977 an interview was recorded with Ted Wheeler who had served for a few years as Clerk at Tintern Station. We sat in his living room at Portskewett and for two hours he talked with great pride and nostalgia about his life as an employee with the Great Western Railway:-

"I went there to work for the railway in 1929. But my association with Tintern Station went back considerably before that. I was born in 1904 and at that time my father kept the old Globe Inn in Tintern. It was only a beer house and there was also a little shop on the side and out in the front there was a yard, where they used to sell coal. Well, occasionally my father would go to Tintern Station to fetch a load of coal and he would take me with him. So from about 6 to 7 years of age, I was familiar with Tintern Station.

The first stationmaster I can remember at Tintern was a man by the name of Hibbert and I can recall him well, because on one occasion that I was up at the station, I picked up a fountain pen. Now that was in the days when a fountain pen was a fountain pen - not a biro you know. I was so pleased, but I had been brought up very strictly at home - my father was a great churchman. Honesty was the main thing that you were taught in those days. So I took the pen to the stationmaster, thinking in my innocent way that if nobody claimed it then it would be returned to me. After some time I heard nothing about it and I then asked at Tintern Station if anybody had claimed the pen. I was politely told that I had no claim on it and it had gone to the lost property office of the Railway.

I went to school in Tintern up to the age of thirteen and then I was fortunate to win a scholarship to Monmouth School. I went to school on the train, which was very enjoyable, but I was never happy there because it was such a bad time. My father was called up to the army in the first war. His business went to pot and my mother wasn't very healthy. He lost everything while he was away and I used to go to school and get so depressed - wondering how things were at home.

A boy in school knew how fed up I was and said to me one day, 'There's a job going, Wheeler, if you would like to apply for it.' 'What's that?' I asked. 'On the Railway,' he said, 'I was thinking of going for the job myself, but my scholarship is issued by the School Governor here and the headmaster won't let me leave.' Well, I was fifteen and my scholarship was under the management of the County Council which meant that I could leave. Unbeknown to mother, I wrote off and soon had an interview and went before the doctor for the medical. I got the job before I told her anything about it.

When my father came home from the war he went into Chepstow Shipyard which was still working then. But two years later the depression started and he was then on the dole for years and years. There was no work at all.

By that time (about 1929) the motor car had come in and the two hotels in Tintern then were the Beaufort Arms and the Anchor and the type of people they used to attract were people of some substance. They didn't just come for the day, they used to come for a fortnight, or three weeks or even a month.

There were always people coming to the station by train and going away, having spent time at the hotels. There were six cars on the cab rank at one time and we were very busy. You must realise that the type of people we dealt with were gentry.

I remember very well when I came there having worked first at a station in the South Wales Valleys, and of course they say that you take on the character of the people that you live with. Anyway, this old gentleman came to the window at Tintern and he asked for a first class single to Paddington and I gave him the ticket and took the money. He then said to me, 'Which way do I go?' Well, there was of course two ways in which he could possibly go, but I unthinkingly said, 'Well, your route is on the ticket'. The old gentleman didn't like that at all. He expected me to tell him. My boss was standing just behind me, and he walked up to me after the old gentleman had gone and said, 'We don't deal with people at Tintern like that Mr Wheeler, you are not in South Wales now!'

Perhaps I could tell you an amusing story against myself. I expect that you know Catchmays Court. Well, the chap living there then was a Mr Perry and he was the representative of Seager Evans the spirit people.

He used to employ a chauffer to bring him to the station. His hobby was breeding poultry. Anyway Jane and I got married on November 2nd, 1929 and about 7 weeks later, we came to Christmas.

I remember Mr Perry getting off the train at 3 o' clock in the afternoon and he called the Governor up. The Governor later returned with several bottles of drink - sherry, port and all. He told us that Mr Perry had kindly left them for the staff and that he would pop up to the house and get some glasses. Well at that time I was a teetotaller - I didn't drink at all. Anyway I had a couple of these ports in tumblers and was talking and talking my head off. The train had just gone up to Monmouth and was on its way back. So I started to book up the passengers for the next train. Of course the ticket case was swinging this way and swinging that way and I couldn't do a thing about it.

I shouted across to the signalman, 'I'm going home Charlie'. 'Alright,' he said. I jumped on my bike and somehow managed to get home. It was a month after I had got married and I fell in through the door drunk as a lord.

I went to sleep for an hour or so and when I woke up I remembered that I had left all the cash and the keys out at the Station. So I rode furiously back there, but found that my boss had sorted everything out. He was like a father to me.

In those days they used to run excursion trains **to** Tintern and **from** Tintern. Would you believe it when I tell you, we used to have an excursion go from Tintern to Weston Super Mare and we used to go by train to Chepstow; walk down from Chepstow Station to where the Fairfield is now and the old *Westward Ho* boat would be waiting there. You would go across the Severn to Weston and back in the evening and catch the train back from Chepstow to Tintern."

"Did any accidents happen on the line during your time there?" I asked.

"Well, I don't remember any real accidents, except for one particular night. We were coming back from Chepstow and we were told that there had been an accident up the Wye Valley and that we couldn't go home that way. We had to go a round-about way and down to Tintern. What had happened was - there had been a fall of rock on the other side of the tunnel from

Tintern Station. It had fallen on the line and blocked it."

"Can you remember any famous people travelling on the line?" I asked.

"Yes, when I was clerk at Tintern, Raphael Sabatini was living at Brockweir House. He was a very famous author who wrote Captain Blood and various historical novels like that. He was a wonderful writer. He of course used to come to Tintern Station and travel on the train and we got to know him very well. He gave the Governor a copy of his book - *Captain Blood*. Sabatini lived at Brockweir for several years and he had a son who was in his twenties and was a bit of a rip like - even for those days - fast cars and so forth. He was driving from Tintern to Llandogo on this particular day when a dog ran across the road. He tried to avoid it but crashed into a tree and was killed. After that the old chap sold up everything and went away.

I remember two old ladies coming here, who were ladies in waiting to Queen Alexandra. They were two sisters - the Honourable Misses Montmorency, and were very tall and distinguished looking. My boss, Mr Davies - he was a dry old stick, said, 'You know who those two old ladies are Mr Wheeler. They are not very nice looking are they?'

'No,' I said, 'they look very staid and stern'.

'Aye,' he said, 'that is because King Edward was a terror for the ladies.' Queen Alexandra used to pick very plain ladies-in-waiting!"

"Where were you living at this time?" I asked.

'I came to Tintern Station as a single man, but within 12 months I got married and got a little cottage down by the Abbey, belonging to my uncle. It had been in my family for many years and it was called Ship Cottage. Round about the turn of the century, the Duke of Beaufort got into financial difficulty and he had to sell part of his estate. It was the Tintern area that was sold you see, and it was turned over to the Crown. Well now, over a period of time when the Abbey became a ruin, if anybody wanted to build a house they would go to the Abbey, pinch the stone and build a cottage. Well of course that was alright when the old Duke was the landlord, but as soon as the Crown took it over they wanted their rent you see, and they went round and started getting rent from all these cottages. But anyhow, this particular cottage belonged to my uncle and they tried to buy that. But he wouldn't sell. 'As long as I own that cottage,' he said, 'they own part of it and I own part of it.'

After living for six years at Ship Cottage, we then moved into Station House at Tintern. Of course that was the first Station House that was built there. I've been trying to remember what happened to the stationmaster before that house was built which was around 1928. We lived there because the stationmaster was a bachelor. He didn't want the house so I applied for it as we had two kiddies and we went to live there.

The engine drivers were wonderful characters. Once they came off the main line at Wye Valley Junction, they were a law unto themselves. I know there were rules and regulations, but what could go wrong on a line like that. Only one train could be running at a time and there was no fear of a collision. They were really wonderful days. You would see that train coming down to Chepstow and when it came back up the valley there would be bean sticks and pea sticks all tied on top of the engine for their allotments.

Ted the Signalman was another interesting character. He would look at his watch and say, 'Time I was on the platform to exchange the staff, which is a sort of token that is used on single track railways.' Over he would come with the staff under his arm - very important man he was. He came stalking over and often he used to come early and help the porter with the luggage and share the tip - he was artful you see. One day he came over from his box as the train came out of the tunnel. But the brakes came on and she came to a dead stop. He had forgotten to pull the signals off!

Back in the old days everything that was sold in Tintern shops came into the station. There were no buses or cars or anything then. There were two carting agencies. They would go into the Station and load up with stuff from the goods shed and take it into the village. They would get commission on that and there was another man who had a cab on the cab rank who used to deal with all the parcels that came in by passenger train and he would get commission on that.

Livestock used to be taken on the train for Monmouth Market and that was quite an event. The farmers would be there in the morning for the quarter past eight train and two of them would perhaps be sharing a waggon.

The train would come in and the cattle waggon would be in the bay. They had to pull it out by hand and the train would back on to it and away she would go. The same thing would happen for the down train to Chepstow.

My uncle used to drive the wagonette to Tintern Station. There were four people in Tintern with such vehicles. My Uncle, a chap named Viner, a man named Jones and one other. They all used to stand in the rank with their horse and wagonette. It had a high seat in the front for the driver and for one more to sit beside him. At the rear it was much lower and you could seat three people each side and there were two steps at the back to get up.

Well they would go up to Tintern Station and wait for the train to come in and I think they charged 6d for a trip to the Abbey. Yes, it was a standard charge for people getting off the train. Now in those days there were also a few wagonettes coming out from Chepstow and of course they could bring people out to Tintern but they couldn't go down to the station because they had to pay the railway cab rent. So they would go along the top road above the station and undercut the locals by shouting down, '3d to the Abbey from here sir!' Yes, there was a proper war between the Chepstow men and the Tintern chaps.

The people of Brockweir and Tintern never got on either for there was a lot of rivalry in those days. Tintern was in Monmouthshire and Brockweir was where the Foresters lived - in a different country. But I lived in Brockweir myself, during the war and found them to be wonderful people with a great sense of humour. There was one old chap who lived on the Monmouthshire side of the river but used to drink in the Brockweir Inn. At closing time he used to say, 'Oh well, I'm going home now - I'm going by rail.' He used to hang on to the hand rail as he staggered over Brockweir Bridge to get home.

I was the last clerk at Tintern Station for I was made redundant. Would you believe it, I must have been the first man working for the Great Western Railway to be made redundant. We then moved to Chepstow, where I worked until 1953 and then we had a staff commission come round trying to cut down on these jobs and I got moved to Portskewett. The first year I came here I must

have had to deal with every accident in the book; sewer slides, fatal accidents, runaways, breakaways - you name it! But I must have handled these problems alright because there were never any complaints.

My son then went to Tintern as relief stationmaster. He became stationmaster at the age of 23 and soon afterwards went away to London to work.

I enjoyed my work and when I finished in 1964 I was really broken-hearted."

"What do you think of Tintern Station now?" I asked.

"I think they've done a marvellous job. If anybody had told me then that they could bring it back to how it is now then, I would not have believed them. I think that it is a credit to all concerned."

Left: *Station Master at Tintern Station.*

South Wales Railway

The first attempt to link the South Wales ports with London was the Bill promoted in 1844, which provided for a route crossing the Severn to Chepstow, and running to Fishguard Bay, which was later altered to a terminus at New Milford.

In 1850, the first section was opened between Chepstow and Swansea, having been constructed by Isambard Kingdom Brunel. The subsequent opening of the Severn Railway Bridge provided a through line to London via Gloucester and the Great Western Railway. But it was not until Brunel completed the Chepstow bridge in 1852 that direct railway communication with London was established. An alternative route to Bristol and the south-west of England was provided in 1863 by the steamer from Portskewett Pier on the Monmouthshire side to the New Passage Pier at Aust. This service was started in 1863 but came to an end three years later when the Severn Tunnel opened. Bristol was linked with London by the Great Western Railway at an early date and it became an important railway centre before the end of the first half of the nineteenth century. In 1863 the South Wales Railway was absorbed by the Great Western Railway Company and converted to Brunel's broad gauge. This became the chief subject of controversy in railway engineering and in due course the decision went against Brunel and the narrow gauge was selected as standard throughout Britain. This meant that the gauge of the South Wales Railway had to be changed - at great expense in 1872. The distance from Monmouthshire to London and Bristol was further shortened in 1886 by the opening of the Severn Tunnel, which brought Newport one hour nearer to London.

The Severn Tunnel

Construction was commenced in 1880 by Thomas Walker, whose tender for the work was the only one received. He worked under the direction of Sir John Hawkshaw. The contractor had to fight against a series of difficulties which were greatly increased by the huge quantity of water from subterranean springs which unceasingly flowed into the workings. The average amount of water pumped out daily exceeded 24 million gallons.

The statistics for the construction of this tunnel are most impressive. No less than 76 million bricks were used, for it is lined with brickwork 3 ft. thick throughout. It is 25 ft. high with a width of 26 ft. The average number of men engaged in the work, at the same time was over 3,000.

The length of the construction from the Monmouthshire side to the Gloucestershire side is 7 miles, while the tunnel itself measures 4 miles, 628 yards. It lies 100 ft. below the bed of the channel at its deepest part and is 145 ft. under the level of high water at spring tide. The fan ventilating the tunnel is 40 ft. in circumference.

Twelve Cornish pump engines kept the tunnel free from water. In November 1961 these Victorian beam engines were replaced by electrically operated submersible pumps.

The tunnel was completed in 1886 at a cost of £2,250,00. It opened for goods traffic on 1 September 1866 and the first passenger train to South Wales passed through the tunnel on 1 July 1887.

Brunel's Bridge, Chepstow

This tubular railway bridge over the Wye at Chepstow was designed by Isambard Kingdom Brunel. Construction commenced in 1849 and a single line was opened on 19 July, 1852. The second line was opened on 18 April of the following year.

Before this bridge was built the South Wales Railway ended on each side of the river and passengers had to make a connection between sections by travelling in a stage coach over the Wye Bridge.

Built at a cost of £90,000 this was the first iron bridge to be designed by Brunel and it involved some new engineering features. In particular each track was supported by an iron tube 100 yards long. It is of interest that the bridge was manufactured in Chepstow by Edward Finch who subsequently invented the first metal mast to be used in the British navy. Brunel's famous ship, the Great Western was also fitted with iron masts, and these were made in Chepstow.

Brunel's design for the Chepstow bridge was a modification of the suspension technique. It was necessary for him to allow for the passage of a considerable volume of river traffic, transporting timber and various products of local industries. At that time the Wye was navigable up to Brockweir by vessels of sixty tons and by barges of forty tons as far as Monmouth. To meet these conditions the Admiralty stipulated a clear headway of 50 ft. above high water mark and a span of not less than 800 ft. above mid-channel.

In the 1960s it was decided that the bridge had become unsafe and it was strengthened by the replacement of the 300 ft. iron tubes by new trusses underneath. These were machine-welded in the adjoining shipyard of the Fairfield Engineering Company. They were then assembled on site with high strength bolts, without interfering with the train services running above.

Above: This tubular railway bridge spanning the Wye at Chepstow was the first iron bridge designed by Isambard Kingdom Brunel and it was opened in July 1852.

151

STONE AND STEAM IN THE BLACK MOUNTAINS

Above: *Grwyne Fawr Valley in the Black Mountains.*

For many years the late Rev David Tipper, vicar of St. Mary's, Balderstone, near Rochdale visited the Black Mountains on walking holidays and became fascinated with the story of the Grwyne Fawr Reservoir which supplies the Western Valley of Gwent with water. Originally it had been forecast that the reservoir would be completed within 40 months, but the Great War intervened and the workforce was taken away.

David Tipper decided to write a book on this project and spent many years researching the background to this fascinating story. He delved into the records of the Gwent Water Board, the minutes of the former Abertilley Water Board and back numbers of the South Wales Argus. He also tracked down and talked to people who had lived at Blaen-y-Cwm and worked on the scheme.

It was of particular interest to him, being an ex-railway man that in connection with this project a line had been built into the heart of the Black Mountains. It was never officially authorised because theoretically it was considered impossible to operate.

However it had to be built to take the men and materials to the remote village of Blaen-y-Cwm, below the construction site of the Grwyne Fawr Reservoir. The line was 11 miles in length and linked with a junction on the GWR line near Llanfihangel station and remained in operation for fifteen years. It was a railway 'of a very exceptional nature, rising to 1,168 ft. in only 11 miles.'

In February 1913 they began to lay the track from Lower Cwmyoy and by April the rail head was into Partrishow with six miles to go. By July, 1919, the trains were running within half a mile of the workers' huts at Blaen-y-Cwm.

The locos 'ANITA' and 'DUCKINFIELD' were the first to work the line. In due course the rail stock grew and later included the locos 'BRIGG' and 'ABERTILLERY 1, 2, and 3. The single line railway was operated without signals on the 'sight and sound' principle of warning. The engines had to be worked hard on the steep inclines, and in the quiet valley the train could be heard for several miles.

All the trucks and 'coaches' were loose, coupled by chains with the inevitable snatchings and jerking movements. Braking was sometimes effected by putting oak sprags through the carriage wheels in the good old 'wild west' style. Brake power was always a problem.

When descending the inclines the locomotive would be put into reverse and given steam so that it worked against the load and acted as a brake. More often the hand brake was fully applied but this simply locked the wheels and the engine slid down the gradient.

Below: *'Duckinfield', one of the first locomotives to be operated on the Grwyne Fawr railway.*

Right: *'Anita' was a general purpose locomotive, kept at Blaen-y-cwm shed and worked 14 hours per day. These locomotives were all maintained in first class condition and painted green with red buffer bars and lined out in red, yellow and black.*

Right: *'Brigg' was purchased by the Water Board in 1919 from the Ministry of Munitions for £1,000.*

KEY

- ———— ROAD
- ·········· RAILWAY
- — — — ROAD AND RAILWAY
- - - - - TRACK

THE ROUTE

Map labels:
TO TALGARTH
TO HAY
GRWYNE FAWR RESERVOIR
FFWDDOG RIDGE
HATTERRALL RIDGE
CAPEL-Y-FFIN
BLAEN-Y-CWM
GADER RIDGE
2624' PEN Y GADER FAWR
LLANTHONY
N
ALLT MAWR RIDGE
TABERNACLE
PARTRISHOW
QUEEN'S HEAD INN
GELLI-WELLTOG
LOWER CWMYOY
PONT ESGOB
LLANBEDR
FFOREST
SUGAR LOAF
BRYN ARW
BETTWS
PEN-Y-CLAWDD
LLANFIHANGEL CRUCORNEY
PANT-Y-GELLI
TO HEREFORD
TO ABERGAVENNY
GREAT WESTERN RAILWAY

Left: *Map showing the route of the Grwyne Fawr railway which ran into the heart of the Black Mountains.*

Below: *View from the top of the dam 28 March 1928.*

155

Right: *Quarry at the far end of the reservoir site..*

The journey from Llanfihangel to the Works took one hour with a maximum speed of 20 mph and an average speed of 12 mph. Remarkably there were no serious accidents on the railway, though the farmer at Llwyncelyn once claimed £3 10s 0d 'for a ewe killed by the locomotive.'

Bad weather was always a hazard. Rain and mountain mist made the rails greasy and snow blocked them. At one time a wedge shaped snow pusher was mounted on a bogey and attached to the locomotive BRIGG in an attempt to clear the dtifts. However, this was not effective and after a blizzard it was a case of every man out with the shovels.

The engines were all maintained in first class condition and Bob Gibson the foreman fitter, had them painted green with red buffer bars and lined out red, yellow and black.

Bill Paine of Llanfihangel had charge of the maintenance of the railway and the road. In all there were approximately twenty miles of track which provided employment for two gangs of plate layers.

At the far end of the reservoir was a quarry with cranes and rock blasting equipment. Some of the quarry workers travelled over the mountain from Talgarth to work at the site.

A few lodged in the village during the week, but as this was an extra expense, others made the double journey each day, performing incredible feats of endurance.

Leaving at 4.00 am men would ride or push their bicycles to the foot of the mountain and leave them there. They would then make a 1,000 ft. ascent up Rhiw Cwmstabl which was followed by a two mile mountain track to the quarry at the northern end of the Reservoir site. Their ten hour shift ended at 5.30 pm and they would return to their bicycles and freewheel most of the way back to Talgarth. Mist, rain and blizzards often made the journey extremely hazardous.

The work force as a whole consisted of a variety of craftsmen and labourers including stonemasons, navvies, the black gang, carpenters and blacksmiths. Most of these men lived at the village and travelled to the reservoir site by train.

From the reservoir side of the dam wall was a twin-sided concrete hoist towering 200 ft. above the ground. Four 2-ton electric travelling cranes were seated on rails on top of the wall, and in 1924, a cable way was fixed across the valley, above the concrete hoist. The span was 11,000 ft., the centre being 250 ft. above the valley bottom. It was christened 'Blondin' after the famous French tightrope walker.

Right: *Contruction of the dam.*

In November 1926 it was decided to extend the railway to the top of the dam and by September 1927 the work was completed. It had involved building a new bridge over the stream near the fitting shops. The train stopped near the fitting shops, reversed over the bridge and pushed the carriages up a half mile incline to the level of the new roadway. Here it reversed again and went forward towards the quarry. In doing so the train crossed the 1,800 ft. contour line, the highest altitude reached by an adhesion-worked railway locomotive in the British Isles.

The workers' village was built two miles below the reservoir site at Blaen-y-cwm. The huts were made of wood covered outside with corrugated iron and apparently they were very snug in winter.

From their appearance the village became known as 'Tin Town' but the Water Board referred to it as 'Navvy Village'. A school was built on the west bank of the Grwyne with a footbridge providing access from the village. It had two class rooms, one for the junior mixed and one for the senior mixed and could accommodate sixty children.   Mr and Mrs Vincent Feathers were appointed as staff and the school officially opened on 18 May 1914. By 1924 the attendance figure had exceeded 40 and by September 1926 it was 49. Teaching was sometimes hampered by gales which shook the building and overnight frosts which froze the ink ! The next addition to the village was a hospital. It consisted of two wards, a surgery, a consulting room and living quarters for a nurse.

157

Dr Hincks who practised at Hay-on-Wye was the Blaen-y-Cwm panel doctor and his visits to the village involved a daunting 10 mile ride over the Gospel Pass to Capel-y-Ffin and then over the top of the Ffwddog ridge and down to the village. In 1915 he left the practice and went off to war, but returned to take up his duties again in June 1919, now making the journey from Hay to Pont Esgob by car and from there by train to Blaen-y-cwm.

By 1925 the village had a population of over 400 men, women and children. Most of the men who took their wives to the Village turned them into boarding house landladies. For example, one of the larger huts had a family of six living at one end, whilst up to 25 lodgers slept in a communal bedroom at the other end.

The one-family huts were located at the upstream or 'posh' end of the village. The accomodation also included a staff hut for members of the office staff who did not have their wives with them. This was well appointed and included a bedroom for the important folk who had to stay overnight such as Dr Hincks and Canon M.E. Davies.

During the 1920's an overnight stay at the Village was quite an experience. The one street (a railway line) was lit with electric lights and by 1923 all the buildings had interior lights. The outside world still used oil and gas lighting. Blaen-y-Cwm even had electricity before Abergavenny!

The railway not only carried the workmen to and from the village, but also ran a 'landladies' special on Tuesdays and a Saturday mail service. It was a complete community, affectionately known as 'Tin Town'. The village was self-contained, with its own school, hospital, church, jail, stores, canteen, recreation rooms, sub-post office, allotments, and even its own football team and male voice choir.

The large Recreation Hall contained a stage for concerts, a billiard table, darts, dominoes, cards etc. Later a wireless and loudspeaker were installed. Dances were held each week with Bill Pattimore at the piano and once a month a dance band from Abergavenny provided the music.

An Annual Sports Day was held on a piece of flat ground below the village. The occasion required a special train to bring up the spectators, hauled by a neatly decorated locomotive. Then followed the races, jumps, tug o' war, tilt the bucket etc. until everyone was tired out.

At last the project was reaching completion and the opening ceremony was fixed for 28 March 1928. Two decades had passed since the scheme had been conceived and by now only one member of the original Committee was still serving and able to travel to the site, and to him, Councillor David Lewis J.P. fell the honour of opening the reservoir.

On that very special day the Grwyne Fawr Light Railway carried its heaviest ever passenger traffic. Nearly 400 people were conveyed to the top of the reservoir in two trains and the completion of this amazing project was celebrated in fine style.

By the end of the year the village had almost disappeared. The canteen was sold to the Hope Baptist Church, Cross Keys, for use as a school room. A widow purchased the schoolmaster's house and had it re-erected opposite Llanbedr church in the adjacent Grwyne Fechan valley. It has since been encased with pre-cast concrete blocks and is now fortunately much more attractive.

Early in 1929 the Grwyne Fawr Light Railway was no more. The land formerly occupied by the railway between the depot at Cwmyoy and Llanfihangel yard was restored to the farmers and landowners.

On 14 June 1930 a newspaper reporter re-visited the works and wrote that the 'railway had gone.' Everything else went with it. The Board demolished the village of Blaen-y-Cwm and the works at the reservoir site. A Birmingham firm paid £3,300 for four locomotives, the railway track, concrete hoist and scrap metal. Local farmers bought the carriages for use as store rooms and chicken pens and the railway sleepers can still be found serving as gate posts.

Today there is no sign of ugly iron or pipework above ground. With a thoroughness that would have delighted the conservationist, they took their 'litter' with them, leaving only the water and a fine public road into the hills.

The Grwyne Fawr dam and reservoir remain as a permanent monument to this project of British engineering and perseverence. Fifty years after the official opening on 28 March 1928, a golden jubilee celebration was held to commemorate the sixteen year period of the reservoir's construction.

Right: Locomotive with the dam wall in background..

IMPORTANT RAILWAY DATES FOR MONMOUTHSHIRE

1804   Richard Trevethick's engine becomes the first ever to run on rails on the Pen-y-Darren Tramroad between Merthyr and Abercynon on February 20.

1829   Samuel Homfray's 'Britannia' takes a trial run from Tredegar to Newport.

1845   Monmouthshire Canal Company obtains an Act of Parliament to improve its tramroads and to build a railway from Newport to the head of the canal at Pontnewynydd, with a branch line to the docks at Newport.

1846   An Act is passed for a Newport, Abergavenny & Hereford Railway.

1848   Monmouthshire Canal Company becomes Monmouthshire Railway & Canal Company.

1850   Monmouthshire Railway & Canal Company order that horse traction is to cease in the Western Valleys and locomotive power only is to be used.
First main line passenger train reaches Newport on June 18 when the broad gauge line of the South Wales Railway from Chepstow to Swansea was opened.

1852   The 10 mph speed limit is abolished.
Dock Street Station is opened as the Newport terminus Western Valley passenger trains running to Blaina, with a branch from Aberbeeg to Ebbw Vale. A single line is opened from Marshes Turnpike Gate, Newport to Crane Street Pontypool.
Brunel's bridge over the Wye on the Great Western route at Chepstow is opened on 19 July.

1853   A new station is opened at Mill Street, Newport.
Monmouthshire Railway Company opens a line connecting Blaenafon directly with Newport.
Work commences on Crumlin viaduct.

1854   An extension is opened to Pontnewynydd.
Passenger trains start to run from Blaenafon to Newport.
Newport, Abergavenny & Hereford Railway opened from Coedygric junction to Hereford.

1855   Tramroads owned by the Monmouthshire Railway and Canal Company are converted into railways during the period 1855-60.

1856   Railway between Little Mill and Usk is opened on 1 June.

1857   Continuation to Monmouth Troy Station is opened.
Official opening of Crumlin viaduct on 1 June.

1858   An impressive stone railway viaduct, with fifteen arches is built on a curve to carry the Great Western Railway, Pontypool to Blaenavon line at Abersychan.

1860   Brecon & Merthyr Company purchase the old Rhymney tramroad and convert it into a railway. The Sirhowy tramroad also become a railroad.
Newport, Abergavenny & Hereford Railway becomes part of the West Midland Railway.

1862   Merthyr Tredegar & Abergavenny Railway opens - single track from Abergavenny to Brynmawr.
Act for a Vale of Crickhowell Railway is passed to provide a line from Abergavenny to Crickhowell.

1864   MT&A Railway - Brynmawr to Nantybwch section is opened on 1 March.

1865   Passenger service starts on the Sirhowy Valley line.

1866   Wye Valley Railway is authorised on 10 August
M.T. & A. Railway is absorbed by L&NWR

1867   Ebbw Vale branch line is opened as a single track.

1870   Cwmffrwdoer and Cwmnantddu branch lines from Pontnewynydd are constructed.
L&NWR Station is opened at Blaenafon in January.

1871   M.T.& A. Railway Nantybwch to Rhymney Bridge section is opened 5 September.

1872   Act to build the Severn Tunnel is passed.
Conversion from broad gauge to standard gauge in South Wales Region.

1873   M.T.&A. Railway Rhymney Bridge to Dowlais section is opened 1 January.

1874   Pontypool, Caerleon and Newport Railway is opened for goods traffic on Sept 18.
Construction of Wye Valley Railway commences .GWR completes its line via Caerleon to Cwmbran.

1875   Sirhowy Valley Railway is taken over by the L&NWR.

1877   MT & A is converted to double track.

1878   GWR opens a connecting branch between Llantarnam Junction on the Caerleon line and Cwmbran Junction on the Monmouthshire line.

1879   Branch line from Pontypool (Trevethin Junction) to Talywaun is opened on 18 September.
MT& A Railway Penywern Junction to Morlais Junction opens on 1 January.

1880   Amalgamation of Monmouthshire Railway & Canal Company with the Great Western system on 1 August.

1886   First train passes through Severn Tunnel on 5 September.

1905   Amalgamation of Wye Valley Railway with GWR.

1922   NLR is amalgamated with the L&NWR on 1st January.

1923   L&NWR ceases to exist, having been taken over, along with the Midland, the Furness, the Glasgow & South Western, and the Highland Railways, by the London, Midland & Scottish Railway.

1941   Waenafon Station closes to passengers on 5 May.

1954   Blaenafon to Brynmawr railway closes on 23 June.

1958   Abergavenny - Brynmawr railway closes.

1959   Wye Valley Railway closes to passengers on 5 January.
Ebbw Vale branch line closes.

1963   Publication of Beeching plan.

1964   Wye Valley Railway closes to goods traffic.

1970   Tintern Station is purchased by Monmouthshire County Council.

1973   The only remaining passenger lines in Monmouthshire are the South Wales main line along the seaboard and the line to the north which runs for 26 miles through the middle of the county from Newport to Abergavenny.

MUSEUMS AND VISITOR CENTRES

Abertillery & District Museum
Situated on the ground floor of the Town's Metropole Theatre, and run by volunteers, this museum has a large collection of artifacts dating from prehistoric times to the 20th century. Open from 10am-4pm, Mondays to Fridays and 10am-2.00pm on Saturdays. Tel: (01495) 2111140.

Big Pit National Mining Museum, Blaenafon
This Museum was opened on the site of the Big Pit Colliery when it closed in 1980. On the colliery surface workshops can be visited and colliery craftsmen can be seen at work. But the highlight of a visit to Big Pit is the descent of the shaft in the miners' cage for an underground tour led by ex-miners. The site is open between 9.30 and 5.00pm daily from the beginning of March to the end of November. Underground tours start at 10.00am and last admissions are at 3.30pm. Tel: (01495) 79031.

Blaenafon Ironworks & Tourist Information Centre
The best preserved 18th Century ironworks in Western Europe is open daily from April to the end of October. Monday to Friday 9.30am-4.30pm, Saturday 10am-5pm/Sunday 9.30am-4.30pm. Visits at other times can be arranged for special interest groups. Telephone Tourism Section, Torfaen County Borough Council (01633) 648082.

Drenewydd Museum, Butetown
Located just off the A465 Heads of the Valleys Road on the A469 at Butetown near Rhymney, this fascinating museum is housed inside two former ironworks cottages. Opening hours: Daily 2pm-5pm. For further information contact the Merthyr Tydfil Heritage Trust. Tel: (01685) 843039.

Eliot Colliery, New Tredegar
The Winding House and the Steam Winding Engine of this now vanished colliery has been preserved by the local council with assistance from the National Museum of Wales. The building contains the last remaining twin-tandem compound winding engine in South Wales. For further information contact the Tourism Officer. Tel: (01443) 815588.

Fourteen Locks, Canal Centre, Newport
Situated in Cwm Lane, just off the A467, this small visitor centre houses a display which tells the story of the Monmouthshire Canal. A trail leads from the centre around a fascinating system of locks and ponds which were constructed to enable the narrow boats to ascend a total height of 168' within just half-a-mile. Tel: (01633) 894802.

Griffithstown Railway Musesum
Housed in a former Great Western Railway Goods Shed is a remarkable collection of railway memorabilia and model railways. Open most days between 9.30am and 5.30pm. Tel: (01495) 762908.

Pontypool and Blaenafon Railway Society
A private steam railway operated by enthusiasts. Trains run every Sunday and Bank Holiday Mondays during the summer. Follow the signs to Big Pit. Tel (01495) 792263.

Newport Transporter Bridge
This fascinating bridge is a fine piece of engineereing and was first suggested in 1898. It was designed by F. Arnedin (who built the famous Marseilles Transporter Bridge) and R.H. Haynes. It was opened by Lord Tredegar on 12 September 1906 and cost £98,000. For more details contact the Transporter Visitor Centre (01633) 257302.

Old Station, Tintern
This is a countryside visitor centre based on an old Victorian railway station, beautifully situated in the heart of the Wye Valley. An exhibition tells the story of the Wye Valley Railway and an audio visual presentation is also available, featuring a journey on the line between Chepstow and Monmouth. Open 1 April-31 October. Tel (01291) 689566.

Pontypool Museum
An interesting museum housed in the Georgian stable block of Pontypool Park House. The displays tell the story of the Torfaen Valley and its people from earliest times to the present day. Open daily from February to December. Tel: (01495) 752036

Risca Museum
Located in the Risca Miners' Institute, adjoining Oxford House Adult Education Centre. The exhibits relate to the industrial and social history of Risca and Gwent as a whole. In particular there is an extensive collection of railway and tramroad artifacts. For information Tel: (01633) 612245.

Tredegar Museum
Located in the Library at the Circle in Tredegar, this small museum was established by Tredegar Local History Society. It contains a wide variety of items associated with the industrial history of the town. Open on Saturdays: 9.30-12.30 and 1.30-4.00pm. Tel: (01495) 723005.

LOCATIONS OF SITES

Angidy Ironworks	ST 529002
Bedwellty House	SO 144085
Big Pit	SO 239088
Blaenafon Ironworks	SO 249093
Brecknock & Abergavenny Canal	SO 298009 to
	SO 045283
British Ironworks	SO 258035
Brunel's Wye Bridge	ST 539941
Butetown	SO 104092
Cefn Golau	SO 138081
Clydach Ironworks	SO 229132
Coed Ithel	ST 527026
Crumlin Viaduct	ST 213985
Cwmbyrgwm Balance Gear	ST 251033
Elliot Engine House	SO 144028
Forgeside	SO 245085
Fourteen Locks	ST 279885
Garnddyrys Forge	SO 258119
Gilwern Aqueduct	SO 244144
Glangrwyne Forge	SO 239161
Glyn Pits	ST 265999
Govilon Wharf	SO 271137
Goytre Wharf	SO 313064
Grwyne Fawr Reservoir	SO 233306
Hill's Tramroad	SO 246116 to
	SO 284131
Keeper's Pond	SO 255108
Llanfoist Wharf	SO 234131
Llanelly Furnace	SO 233138
Llanelly Forge	SO 235140
Newport Transporter Bridge	ST 318863
Pen y Fan Pond	ST 195005
Pontymoile Wharf	ST 294003
Pontypool Park Gates	ST 291005
Pwlldu Tunnel	SO 248097 to
	SO 245116
Rhymney Ironworks	SO 109091
Round Houses Car Park	SO 190102
Sirhowy Ironworks	SO 143102
Smart's Bridge	SO 232128
Talywaun Viaduct	ST 263042
Tintern Station	ST 536006
Trellech Furnace	ST 487048
Tymawr, Nantyglo	SO 190102

SUGGESTED READING

Barber C., *Cordell Country*, Blorenge Books, (1985), (1996).

Barrie D.S., *The Rhymney Railway* , (1952)

Baxter B., *Stone Blocks and Iron Rails* (1956).

Byles A., *The History of the Monmouthshire Railway and Canal Company* , (1982)

Cordell A., *Rape of the Fair Country*, (1959)

Coxe W., *An Historical Tour of Monmouthshire*, (1801)

Davies E.J., *The Blaenavon Story*, (1957)

Gray-Jones A., *A History of Ebbw Vale*, (1971)

Hadfield C., *The Canals of South Wales and the Border* (1960)

Humphreys. G., *Industrial Britain: South Wales*, (1972)

Jones O., *The Early Days of Sirhowy and Tredegar*, (1969)

Lloyd J., *The Early History of the Old South Wales Iron Works, 1760-1840*, (1906)

Morris, J.H. and Williams L.J., *The South Wales Coal Industry 1841-75* (1958)

North F.J., *Coal and the Coalfields in Wales* (1931)

Phillips E., *Pioneers of the South Wales Coalfield* (1925)

Rattenbury G., *Tramroads of the Brecknock and Abergavenny Canal*, (1980).

Rees D.M., *Mines Mills and Furnaces* (1969)

Rees Morgan D., *Industrial Archaeology of Wales* (1975).

Rees Morgan, *Mines, Mills and Furnaces*, (1969)

Scrivenor H., *A Comprehensive History of the Iron Trade* (1841)

Stevens, R. A., *The Brecknock & Abergavenny and Monmouthshire Canals*, (1975)

Tipper, D., *Stone and Steam in the Black Mountains*, (1985)

Van laun J., *The Clydach Gorge*, (1979)

Wilkins C., *The History of the Iron, Steel, Tinplate and other Trades of Wales* , (1903)

OTHER TITLES BY CHRIS BARBER

Walks in the Brecon Beacons

Exploring the Waterfall Country

Ghosts of Wales

Exploring the Brecon Beacons National Park

Exploring Gwent

Mysterious Wales

More Mysterious Wales

Cordell Country

The Romance of the Welsh Mountains

Hando's Gwent

Hando's Gwent Volume Two

The Ancient Stones of Wales (with John G. Williams)

The Seven Hills of Abergavenny

Journey to Avalon (with David Pykitt)

Classic Walks in the Brecon Beacons National Park

Eastern Valley

ACKNOWLEDGEMENTS

This book has been compiled over many years during which time numerous people have given assistance and advice. In particular several experts in their field have passed on their knowledge and experiences during tape-recorded interviews which have helped to ensure the recording of detailed information and personal enthusiasm. In this respect Anne Wilson, Trevor Rowson, Len Burland, Foster Frowen, Lionel Milsom, Colin Read, Glyn Hallett, Graham Gratton and Ted Wheeler (now deceased) are warmly thanked for their assistance.

In addition we would like to thank the staff at The Valley Inheritance Museum, Pontypool, Big Pit, Blaenafon and those employed at the numerous libraries in Gwent who gave valuable assistance. Technical advice was also given by John van Laun, Hugh Phillips and Richard Dommett.

Special thanks are also due to Paul Wellington and Sue Parkinson who read the draft manuscript and made helpful comments. Finally we are most grateful to Sir Richard Hanbury-Tenison for writing the foreword.